'A wee morning blether with TT always brightens up my day. Theresa's humour and enthusiasm for life are so infectious.'
— **KAYE ADAMS**

'Theresa is known to everyone at BBC Scotland. Not in the way that some criminals are 'known' to the Police...

She's friendly, humorous and thoughtful and so is her writing. She seems to use parenthesis a lot (but so do I) (and there's nothing wrong with that).'
— **FRED MACAULAY**

Hey Higgy
there's nothing like
curling up with
a good book.
and this is
nothing like a
good book!

This Is
What I
Look Like

Enjoy.

Theresa Talbot

Theresa xxx.

Published by
Strident Publishing Ltd
22 Strathwhillan Drive
The Orchard
Hairmyres
East Kilbride
G75 8GT

Tel: +44 (0)1355 220588
info@stridentpublishing.co.uk
www.stridentpublishing.co.uk

Published by Strident Publishing Limited, 2014
Text © Theresa Talbot, 2014
Cover photo by Bob McDevitt Photography
Cover design by LawrenceMann.co.uk

ISBN 978-1-905537-84-6

Typeset in Optima by Andrew Forteath | Printed by CPI

ABOUT THERESA TALBOT

Theresa is a freelance writer, journalist and radio presenter. She is perhaps best known for presenting BBC Radio Scotland's *Traffic and Travel* and the weekly gardening programme *The Beechgrove Potting Shed*.

She has also worked as an independent producer and editor, creating programmes for the likes of BBC Radio 2.

Prior to working with BBC Radio Scotland she worked for Radio Clyde, Q96 and AA Roadwatch, though her love of radio all started when she volunteered with Hospital Radio.

And, before she entered the media, Theresa worked in various roles – as an assistant in children's homes, as a Pepsi Challenge girl and as a library assistant.

She ended up at the BBC because of an eavesdropped conversation on a no.66 bus in Glasgow.

Theresa's passions include gardening, music, keep-fit…and rescuing chickens.

ACKNOWLEDGMENTS

A huge thank you to:

Keith Charters who came up with the idea for this book while suffering from man flu and an alleged temperature of 103. His editing skills, general patience and custard creams are greatly appreciated.

My beautiful sister, Tricia Law, who is the best friend I could wish for. She, along with fellow siblings Stephen and Martin, helped create the most precious family memories and had the good grace not to write them down first!

William my 'early reader', Bob McDevitt for the photographs, Max Watson who was happy to let me 'use his head', and my dear friend Susan Dignon who prompted my memory of happy days.

And of course each and every listener who switches on their radio and allows me into their lives for a few minutes each day.

'Thank you' isn't a big enough sentiment for what I feel for Doalty. He believes in me, which isn't quite the same as *believing me!*

But most of all I owe an enormous debt of gratitude to Mum & Dad. They were truly wonderful and always treated me like one of the family!

CONTENTS

For Mum and Dad
….and a dog called Rusty!

PROLOGUE

Last week I bumped into a chap who was in the same year as me at Uni. I hadn't seen him for almost 2 decades, but could tell from his suit, watch and 23-year-old girlfriend that he was loaded and, I therefore assumed, had a brilliant job. We circled and did the usual exchanges, all the while eyeballing each other to see who was galloping into middle age with most dignity. He'd lost some of his hair, but apparently made up for this by not needing glasses; I, on the other hand, have a full head of hair – always a bonus on a woman – but occasionally need glasses when my arms become too short for small print.

His mobile phone was high-spec, high-gloss and probably blue-toothed to NASA; but he didn't know how to work it. Whereas my phone does little more than make calls and let me text my friends to say I'm going to be late, but I gained valuable ground by imparting my superior knowledge and wisdom (it's all relative) to show him how to play pinball on his.

He came right back with a drop kick, nodding with apparent pity when I told him what I do for a living – which is basically talking out loud on the wireless. 'Awww', he said, in a tone normally reserved for asking elderly relatives if they'd like to use the toilet. 'And you showed great promise too. Didn't you win the class prize for Economics?'

I did that mixture of a shrug and an upward nod.

He wasn't letting go. 'I thought you became an accounts executive for a pharmaceutical company when you left Uni?'

I added a 'meh' and an Elvis lip to my shrug and upward nod. 'Wasn't for me,' I replied.

'That's strange,' he said, smiling at the obvious irony of the glittering career which lay behind me. 'I always thought you'd go on to great things. So how on earth did you end up doing traffic reports?'

'I just got lucky I guess!'

THE EARLY YEARS...IN BRIEF

I was born at a very young age in the Royal Maternity Hospital in Glasgow, or the 'Rottenrow' as it was commonly known, after the street in which it stood. The locals quickly took me under their wing and I decided to stay.

***

My first and only ever babysitter was a huge German Shepherd called Rusty. Rusty would guard my pram while I slept outside our tenement block in Finnieston, baring his teeth at anyone who dared approach.

Rusty belonged to my godmother, Ruby, who was considered rather risqué because she 'lived in sin' with Peter The Pole, who ran a card school and speakeasy from their flat one floor below us. Sadly, I have no recollection of Ruby or her dog!

Why my Mother chose Ruby as my godmother – and thus the guardian of my moral welfare in the event of her demise – is anyone's guess. But I'm glad she did. In a way it set my stall out early; it encouraged me to aim for the road less travelled. And *I think* it did me no harm, but perhaps that's for you to judge!

FAMILY, MAPS AND MISHAPS...

For as long as I can remember I've been fascinated by maps. As a child I was left in awe by those twirly-swirly, wiggly lines that joined up villages, towns and people's lives across the country. In our house there was a mystery to maps that yielded power and currency greater than gold. In the days before motorways linked every street and sat-navs gently seduced you into following their directions without question, we went on a family trip from Glasgow to London.

Dad was behind the wheel, while Mum's job was to navigate, the giant AA Road Map perched on her knee. My Mother was nothing if not confident; never one to admit her failings, she barked directions at Dad with the conviction of Boadicea leading her troops into battle, while flailing her arms across his face every so often to punctuate her commands. I sat in the back, mesmerised by her knowledge and power. A weird alchemy took place as she made sense of all those squiggly lines on the page, deciphering colour codes worthy of a Dan Brown mystery and traversing us safely to our destination.

Mum was the brains behind this operation make no mistake. Dad was going like the clappers mind you – working the peddles, keeping the wheel steady and flicking the indicator on and off when corners beckoned

– but we knew Mum was the captain of the ship.

Or so we thought, until nine hours later we ended up in…

…Edinburgh!

The exchange that followed between my (normally) mild-mannered father and my somewhat flamboyant, devil-may-care mum can't be repeated here; we were ordered never to speak of the episode again! But what I *can* tell you was that the road atlas was closed over and we were informed in hushed tones that maps were not to be trifled with. They were to be revered and respected and were probably not for the likes of us. Ordinary untrained individuals had no right messing about with such hallowed tomes.

But it was too late. I was hooked!

SAT-NAVS AND OTHER STRANGE CREATURES...

It must be said that a misguided sense of direction and overinflated opinion of one's ability can afflict even the most competent drivers.

My dad (he of the famed mild-manneredness) failed his driving test first time round. Why? Because when the examiner told him to 'proceed' he pulled away from the kerb and, with all the natural instincts of a homing pigeon, drove straight home, ignoring all other instructions. Clearly he thought the examiner battering the dashboard with a copy of the Highway Code was some sort of signal that all was well.

That's another family episode I swore I would never mention again in public!

But for those of you who think sat-nav has taken the guess work out of driving, let me introduce you to my friend's sister. We'll call her 'Maggie' to protect her identity. (Oh come on, there must be millions of Maggies in Glasgow!)

Maggie has taken to calling her sat-nav 'The Bitch' because of the rude way it insists on interrupting her in-car conversations with such trivial information as *'Turn left'*…. *'You're running out of fuel'* or *'The car is on fire, please exit at the next junction or you will all die'*.

We've told Maggie the device has gender options available – that she can have a male voice or even some minor down-at-heel celebrity – but she's very resistant to change.

During one epic journey from Glasgow to Airdrie, Maggie switched 'The Bitch' to silent mode, leaving her free to chat merrily with – or perhaps that should be 'at' – her 3 gal-pal passengers. (Maggie has an enviable way of chatting merrily even when telling the most gruesome tale.) The 40-minute journey had reached the 90-minute mark, with Maggie ignoring her friends' rumblings of 'are we there yet?' because, despite their tumultuous relationship, Maggie trusted The Bitch implicitly. Every so often she would glance at the screen to make sure she was still on track – and sure enough she was.

'One minute till destination,' she announced as she turned left into the cul-de-sac, then took the third right, straight to what should have been her friend's door.

'Erm, Maggie,' came a voice from the back. 'Why is your husband sitting in [what should have been] Claire's lounge with your dog on his knee?'

Maggie stared through the picture window and sure enough there her husband was, feet up, bold as brass.

The Queen of Double Takes had nothing on Maggie that day. She realised that in her haste to switch off the nagging, relentless voice of the sat-nav she'd also pressed the default 'home' button – the one that is guaranteed to find your house no matter where you are on the planet.

And sure enough, Maggie had driven straight to her *own* front door.

It takes a particular set of skills to make a mistake *that* big.

Maggie did the only thing any decent woman would do. She crouched down with her head out of sight and drove blind as her pals navigated her out of the cul-de-sac.

Owen stared out of the window, slack jawed at the sight of his wife's 'driverless' car miraculously moving of its own accord with Maggie's 3 best pals grinning like crazy and merrily waving to him from the passenger seats.

I can't remember if Maggie swore me to secrecy on that one or not, but in my defence I'm sure her husband Owen has told legions of folk by now.

(Oh come on, there have to be trillions of Maggie/Owen couple combinations out there!!)

PRAISE BE TO ALAN!

After the Glasgow-to-London/Edinburgh episode, I decided it was time to get behind the wheel myself.

The fact that I was only four years old had little bearing on this decision! I'd seen my dad do it. How hard could it be? I knew it would involve a lot of teeth-grinding, gesticulating and puffing on pipes; clearly I was too young to smoke a pipe, but the rest I could master in the safety of my own bedroom before taking to the open road.

I set up my own wee kartie, constructed from an empty drawer. Still in the confines of my bedroom, and with the Campsie Hills in view from the window, I seemed to have a natural gift for driving. Modesty aside, it didn't take that long to learn. I couldn't see what all the fuss was about. I just needed to get myself a set of wheels.

It didn't take too long before the opportunity presented itself.

It arrived in the form of a milk float. 'Praise Be To Alan!' I cried (for that was the milkman's name!) when one Saturday morning I saw he had left his wee truck 'on' while meandering up the garden path to deliver his gold-top.

There was one tiny flaw in my opportunistic plan: it was obvious I needed an accomplice. My feet barely reached the ground, let alone the pedals on Alan's float.

At that moment I spotted Pauline Mills, ages with me and just as tiny. Together we would be able to get the float going. To my surprise she took very little persuading, so I jumped behind the wheel and she crouched underfoot to work the pedals. Quick as a flash we were off.

Oh the thrill of being behind the wheel for real, with the open road stretching out in front, the wind flowing through my hair, the screams of my mother in the background...!

I swear it was her screaming that put me off my stride. Had it not been for that piercing noise I wouldn't have had a momentary lapse in concentration...or hit the kerb...or crashed Alan's pride and joy. And had it not been for that woman's scream I would have been in the Campsies by now.

Alas, dear reader, the milk float overturned and ended up on its side. To this day the sound of breaking glass fills me with dread. Every bottle lay shattered and weeping on the tarmac.

Miraculously, Pauline and I managed to crawl out from the wreckage unscathed. Just a little shaken, by all accounts. Alan, on the other hand, wasn't so lucky. His milk float was a right off. I never did find out if he was recompensed for his ruined cargo.

STEALING IS SUCH AN UGLY WORD!

It was around this same time that I discovered my love of gardening. Perhaps I should call it a passion, for love is a nice, warm, fuzzy feeling of happiness and contentment. Passion on the other hand is wild and wanton and makes you do crazy things completely out of character. Also I was four years old – below the age of reason as any court in the land will tell you. And please don't let the previous mix-up over the milk-float colour your judgement.

Let me put you in the picture and you can make your own mind up.

When I was wee, only posh folk had well-tended gardens. Posh folk with no weans. Their plots were regimented rows of dahlias and hybrid tea roses, neatly under-planted with carpet bedding. And these gardens were often forbidden zones as far as children, football and mad dogs were concerned, all three of which our family had in abundance.

Our garden at the time, although sizeable, consisted of a football pitch (Australian Rules), a rabbit hutch with 10 rabbits and a sprawling raspberry patch. We were allowed to roam wild and carefree in this adult-free oasis, unburdened by cries of 'Oi, get off my lawn'.

I was happy with my lot, until I climbed a rung on the fence and peered into next door's dear green place. I can just about describe what I saw, but nothing can explain the effect it had on me. Instead of a muddy expanse of waste land, before me was an oasis – a veritable paradise with a neatly manicured lawn, flower beds exploding with colour. But what really captured my heart were the perfect vegetable patches – each one boasting row upon row of carrots, broccoli, potatoes. My Beatrix Potter stories had nothing on Mr Reilly's garden.

I don't know what came over me. I knew I couldn't climb the fence but reckoned I could just about crawl under it. (Fagin would have been proud.) Once inside, it just seemed to get easier and easier.

I want you to know that, even with the passage of time, what I am about to reveal still makes me burn crimson with shame.

I pinched Mr Reilly's veg!

I pulled up plant after plant, vegetable after vegetable. The bright orange carrots hypnotised me, the green kale crooked a finger beckoning me closer, just begging to be plucked from the earth...

My plunder was sizeable. It was easy lobbing them over the fence into our garden, then crawling back through to the safety of home.

I don't want you to think this was a random act of vandalism. For I did the decent thing and re-planted each and every piece of contraband in my own garden, expecting the spectacular results that Mr Reilly's years of toil had produced.

Of course my first foray into guerrilla gardening had one flaw... Actually it had many flaws, but the main one was that my crime was in full view of everyone. And now our Australian Rules football pitch was strewn with badly planted wilting greens that were pointing the finger. Clearly the culprit lay under our roof. Poor Mr Reilly (for that was what he was called forever more in our house) came chapping on the door. I have to admit, under the circumstances he was most gracious.

My Mother lined the boys up first. Of course they denied all knowledge. My Sister – who (apart from falling off her platforms in the late '70s) rarely put a foot wrong – wasn't even questioned. I, of course, decided to fess up and admit my deed. After all, what was my crime? Succumbing to an all-consuming passion?

'Eh,' I said as I wriggled through the boys' legs to confront Poor Mr Reilly. 'It was me actually.' My Mother was in a state of near collapse, and all eyes were upon me. 'Well,' I continued in my defence, pointing the finger of blame at Poor Mr Reilly who had suddenly become the guilty party, 'he has loads and loads and loads and is just *greedy*!'

By this time my parents were considering setting up a trust fund, not to pay for my wedding or education (as was the trend with daughters) but to compensate any other poor soul who happened to be in the line of fire when I decided there was a social injustice!

HOLY MATRIMONY
AND FLORAL LARCENY
(or...A Dozen Red Roses and Two Hail Marys
to Go Please!)

I've said that my sister rarely put a foot wrong, but actually the previous story has brought to mind something that happened just a few short years later. Tricia was indeed culpable, but, like my crime, hers was also for the greater good.

In the early '70s we lived in the south side of Glasgow. A local girl was getting married and it was all very rushed. I thought when I heard people say she 'had to get married' she too was gripped by an all-consuming passion and indeed would simply explode if she didn't marry within the month.

The wedding party was to be in her house, with her mother organising some food and drink for a few friends and neighbours. A quiet affair. Anyway, I was too young to help, but when my own mum went up the night before to lend a hand it transpired absolutely nothing had been prepared for the wedding feast the next day. So immediately it was all hands on deck.

Mum and her friend Peggy set to work making steak pies, preparing veg and even baking a wedding cake. Tricia and her best friend Vera (who happened to be

Peggy's daughter) were in charge of setting tables and did a grand job, but come almost midnight there were no flowers. This was long before the days of sumptuous bouquets being available in garage forecourts 24/7.

You know what's coming don't you?

In the dead of night, Tricia and Vera, armed with scissors and poly bags, scoured the neighbourhood for fresh blooms. They must have sneaked into over 50 gardens and covered a 2 mile radius, snipping and plucking and pruning. They returned 2 hours later, looking like a delivery from Interflora, and set about creating the most lavish decorations with the contraband blooms.

Like my misdemeanour before them, they weren't really stealing; it was all for the greater good. Of course, they could never admit to creating the masterpieces lest they got found out.

For their part in the crime, Mum and Peggy said 2 Hail Marys and 5 Our Fathers every day for a month.

SPEED READING AND POWER NAPS

My sister used to say that my CV looked like a sniper's elbow. Tricia can be quite cutting at times, but in fairness I did go through a fair number of jobs before finding my chosen path.

My first job was in a bank. But to be honest I'd rather not talk about that! Suffice to say that I wasn't suited to the banking industry. I'd just left school aged 17, with half a dozen 'O' Grades and a couple of Highers under my belt, and further education was not on the cards. Jobs were plentiful and, unless you wanted to become a teacher, folk from my background didn't go onto University. I rather liked the idea of being a student, to be honest, though mainly because I could then have avoided working in the bank. I think my mum saw through my motives.

I soon left the bank and meandered into Glasgow Libraries, becoming a library assistant. I loved that job. Being surrounded by books and magazines all day and everyday was like a dream come true.

I got to work in several libraries throughout the city and each was different, each had its own charm.

Mosspark library (which I think has long since gone) was a tiny wee building with just two members of staff on duty at any one time. It didn't take long to get to know each person who walked through the door, and they were all so lovely. Actually, some could be quite grumpy, but on the whole the Mosspark residents were just dandy. Some even brought me biscuits and cakes.

But a special mention has to go to a lovely lady who turned up one going-home time with a big rain hat for me. It was during a downpour and when she'd been in earlier I'd mentioned that I'd left my brolly at home.

Isn't that amazing?

I did fall asleep on the job one day though. I swear I was just resting my eyes, but you see it was so warm and cosy in there and the lack of proper windows made for a poor circulation of fresh air… I swear I rested my head on the desk but for a moment. Anyway, so lovely were the readers that they tip-toed past me and queued up outside the Head Librarian's office (a glorified cupboard) to get their books stamped, clearly deciding it would be a shame to wake me.

***

In those days you could renew library books over the 'phone, and one gentleman would telephone each month, as regular as clock-work, to renew his book. I didn't need to know the title of the book, just his name and card number. Alas, after 6 months I told him he'd need to bring it back as there was a limit to how many times a loan could be renewed. True to his word he popped in that very afternoon. 'Jings', he said as he handed it over, 'it's taking me ages to get through that bloody book'. And I burst out laughing when I saw that it was *Speed Reading for Beginners*.

FIRST EDITIONS AND DOG EARS...
AND SOARING OVER BARBARA
CARTLAND

I quickly discovered that libraries were not always the hushed and hallowed buildings we think they are. Keen to show the public that they offered more than just books and a place to shelter from the rain, staff were encouraged to come up with new ideas to entice more people through the doors. (I believe they're called 'service users' now, but we just called them 'people'...)

These ideas became increasingly bizarre. Initially I volunteered to go round local schools and nurseries doing 'storytelling'. No-one else fancied it, but it was a great wheeze – the chance to have a few hours 'off work' and sneak in a spot of guilt-free shopping on my way home.

3-year-olds can be harsh critics, and keeping their attention for any length of time proved to be a bit of a challenge, but it was all good. And my invaluable skill base was growing, because I could now add 'reading story books upside down' to my CV. (Just to be clear, it was the *book* that was upside down as I had to peer over the top to show the children the pictures...it wasn't me standing on my head.)

We also held art exhibitions at the library, as well as short story competitions and even a panto!

But (alas) nothing could top the great 'dog display' fiasco of 1982.

I have no idea whose idea it was to have 5 police dogs visit the library to show off their agility and prowess. My guess is that one of my fellow librarians fancied one of the coppers who used to come in...and saw this as a way to inveigle herself into his affections.

We didn't quite have the facilities in the library to erect a full-size canine assault course. So the 'jumps' had to be improvised. This meant using the free-standing book shelves as hurdles, with a few poor 'mugs' holding plastic hula-hoops for the dogs to jump through. Luckily I'd already done my bit for Queen and Country with the storytelling to ungrateful 3-year-olds, so I was off the hook for that one.

Remember that this was 30 years ago. Then, libraries were places of quiet refuge away from the hurly burly of life; everything was done with a Bic pen, a rubber stamp and a pair of specs dangling round your neck on the sort of natty chain that would now be very 'on-trend' (as I believe the expression goes).

Anyway, we advertised for weeks in advance that the Great Shawlands Dog Show would be coming to the local library. And when the day eventually arrived we were all quite excited, regardless of it being a somewhat dreich Saturday.

Now, I can't remember what part of 'don't feed the dogs' we didn't understand, but as soon as the boys in blue arrived we dispensed tit-bits a plenty, none of which were suitable for dogs. Some say it was this overdose of E numbers that contributed to the subsequent disaster.

Anyway, the display got off to a flying start. All the dogs trotted round the room in single file to 'ooh's and 'aww's from the staff and public alike. Then it was time to pull out the big guns and get them to do the jumps.

No-one had thought to measure the book stands beforehand and we had no idea how high a police dog could actually jump.

Pretty high, as I was soon to discover.

The first dog made it without breaking a sweat. A round of applause rippled through the room. The second dog did likewise, and we let out a collective sigh of relief as his massive bulk soared easily above Barbara Cartland. All was going well.

Dog three was apparently the star of the show and would do the jump *and* glide through the make-shift hula-hoop-come-circus-ring at the same time, like a majestic bird of prey.

I'm not quite sure how to describe what happened next – it all became a bit of a blur. As dog three gained speed – running towards the book case ready for the leap – the librarian holding the hoop took fright at the sight of 80 pounds of German Shepherd thundering towards her. Perhaps it was the bared teeth, or the saliva spraying from his mouth, or the pinned-back ears. Whatever it was, instead of holding the hoop steady she screamed like a banshee and threw it into the air. The poor dog, used to following orders, took this as his cue to leap through the hoop come-what-may, and hurled himself a further 3 feet skywards. In the process, he caught his back paw on the book case and sent an entire Mills & Boon collection crashing headlong into a group of service users.

Meanwhile, a few young boys had come to the attention of two of the ever-vigilant police dogs. The lads had shuffled in out of the rain, but apparently reeked of marijuana. Heady with applause ringing in their ears, the dogs recognised the stench and decided to round up the boys, corral style. They soon had them pinned to the wall by their shoulders and were howling to their handlers for approval. All the while the now hoopless (and hopeless) librarian screeched, while the rest of us ran about like headless chickens telling everyone to keep calm. I might add that *everyone* was calm, it was just us, the members of staff, who were unable to cope with so much excitement on one day.

We flustered about like mother hens, cleaning up – straightening up the book case, dusting down the shocked civilians who had escaped unharmed – and tossing more contraband treats to the dogs. The boys in blue did a hasty retreat, obviously disgusted at our lack of both organisation and stoicism, and the hoopless screeching librarian never did get her date.

***

As an aside, it's worth mentioning that less than a generation before (15 years or so), the 'marriage bar' was still in force for much of the skilled female workforce in the UK. That included librarians, who upon getting married had to leave their posts. It almost beggars belief now, but when I worked for the department there were many 'middle-aged' single female librarians who had forfeited the opportunity to get married or have a family because of their career choice. These bright, pioneering women, who'd studied hard for their 4-year degrees, were forced to make this impossible 'choice'. It makes the archetypical stereotype of the lonely 'spinster' librarian all the crueller. The same employment law was also instrumental in encouraging many women away from university and college education and into lower-paid unskilled work. This is now one of my particular hobby-horses, but I'm ashamed to admit that as a teenager I didn't understand the implications of it.

ALLELUIA: BEHOLD THE BORN-AGAIN STUDENT…

You'll gather that my jobs were many and varied. Although I truly did love my time at the library, after 2 years I felt it was time to move on. With no degree and no real skills (reading story books upside down and reciting the entire script of *The Sound of Music* off by heart – more on that later – would only take me so far) I thought I'd do a spot of travelling.

I reckoned I could back-pack for a few months and when I returned everything would slot into place; my chosen path would open in front of me like the Red Sea parting. In a way it did…if my chosen path was a mish-mash of part-time and temporary jobs. But as I said, this was a different time, when jobs were still fairly thick on the ground. Post-lady, waitress (one day, but it still counts), chauffeur (4 days, but this was only a short-term contract!) promotions girl, Pepsi Challenge Girl (you can see a pattern developing here), aerobics teacher (I actually danced with Lionel Blair for this one. If you're under 50, Google him, he was big in his day). I was even a care assistant in a children's home for some time, which was challenging, fun and heart-breaking all at the same time.

In fact I've lost count of the things I did to scrape a living. None of which looked as though it was forging a career in radio. I actually came to radio very late in life – well, early in my over-all life but late to start a career in the media, which appears to be dominated by 12-year-olds now.

So, when I realised that my string of temporary jobs was leading me nowhere, I did the sensible thing and went back to college to get some more Highers. After which I was lucky enough to get a place at Glasgow University to do an Arts & Social Science Degree. This was pre student loan days, with the luxury of full grants available, otherwise I'd have been snookered. There was no way I could have funded myself through 4 years of higher education and I feel heart sorry for people today who have no choice.

Four years after walking through the doors of Glasgow University I came out with a second class honours degree in Economic History. I thought I was the bee's knees until graduation day when I was in the loo. Above the toilet paper some joker had scrawled *'Social Science Degrees, Please Take One'*. I didn't care, if truth be told. I still thought I was *'it'*.

***

So the day after graduating I woke up and that familiar thought-bubble hung heavy above my head: *'So, what are you going to do for a living?'*

I toyed with the idea of doing a post-grad until my

friends and family yelled a collective, 'Aw come on tae grips!'

I'd met a fabulous girl on my course called Jess. She'd left nursing to go to Glasgow Uni and she was in the same boat as me: she still couldn't work out what her chosen career should be. So we both trotted along to the careers advisor.

George Something (I can't remember his name but he wore a brown jumper) was good, he did exactly what he said on the tin. He spent half an hour with each of us, going through our qualifications with a fine-toothed comb. But with non-vocational degrees, it was our personality types that George said would dictate our futures.

And we believed him. So he ran a battery of tests on us, where we bared our very souls. We were rather excited by all this attention and thought how jolly it would be if we were actually destined for the same career! We could hardly wait for the results.

'Now,' said George Something, tugging his brown jumper down over his expanding tummy. 'This isn't an *exact* science you understand [unlike the social science I had studied, of course], but I like to say I've been pretty accurate over the years.' We stared in agonising anticipation at the paper in his hand, eyes like saucers.

'Jess,' he said, handing over her results first, 'you should try a career in nursing. Theresa', he continued, 'you'd make the perfect librarian!'

'Are you fucking kidding me?' It was the first time in 4

years I'd heard Jess swear.

By this time the tears were streaming down my cheeks at George's crestfallen expression! We both left the careers office and spent the rest of the afternoon in Chimmi Chungas downing Margaritas.

GRAND THEFT DOGGO

One of my favourite jobs was as a care assistant in the Children's Homes. I worked in a couple within Glasgow; two stretches during the long summer holidays in the 1980s as a student and also during a gap year when I realised that even with a full grant I would need extra dough to see me through the harsh winter. So around two years in all. And, as I've said elsewhere, it was rewarding and heart-breaking in equal measures.

What was odd about the whole experience was that, at the tender age of 22, I was 'taken on', with no training and no qualifications and just told where and when to turn up for my first shift! I'd only been dressing myself for 3 years and looked about 12. In fact when I answered the door people would look me up and down and ask, 'Is there a member of staff available?' Yet the council were employing me as a care assistant in a residential home!

Looking back now this actually beggars belief. Especially when one considers the delicate and vulnerable nature of the children who were in my care. I'm sure this wouldn't happen today. I *hope* it wouldn't happen today!

There are a hundred stories I could tell, and I obviously have to be quite circumspect about what I say here – after all there are children's privacy issues to consider. But the other day I was in Tenement House in Glasgow and saw a pair of Wally Dugs[1*] on the mantel piece, which brought back memories...

We used to take the kids down to Haggs Castle in Pollokshields, which was then a Children's Museum. They loved it and it and was a favourite haunt of the staff and weans alike. Anyway, Haggs Castle also had a pair of Wally Dugs among other toys, ornaments and paraphernalia from yesteryear. And one day The Wally Dugs were stolen.

Murder, Polis!

There was mayhem. It was the talk of the steamie.

We had visited the Castle that very morning, but alas had left before the grand larceny took place and thus missed the ensuing excitement. The Dugs were worth quite a lot of money apparently. Despite missing the actual event, we sort of basked in the reflective glory; some claimed to have seen a 'right dodgy looking guy – with a moustache' hanging about; others were sure they had caught a glimpse of the getaway car. Deep down we were fizzing mad at missing this, since not much happened during the summer holidays.

It was even featured on *Crime Desk*! For those of you not fortunate enough to remember the programme, *Crime Desk* was a sort of poor man's *Crimewatch*. As you can

---

1   * Wally Dugs were (normally Staffordshire) glazed pottery dog figurines from Victorian times. They always came in pairs. They were also produced in Glasgow. I think the name 'wally' means 'pale ceramic' as in Glasgow closes with original tiles are described as 'wally closes' (That's where peely-wally must come from too – but that's another story!)

tell from the title, it involved a big desk. Presented by Bill Knox, it was on before the news each evening. Bill, with his headmaster specs and brill-creamed hair, sat behind the eponymous desk, prepped to talk about all sorts of international crime and espionage, but in reality he just spoke about 'local Neds' who'd broken into a bowling club, or who'd defaced a bus-shelter with swearie words. It was the first time we'd ever heard the word Neds used on the telly-box and Bill became a bit of a local celebrity.

(There's a bit of discrepancy as to where the word 'ned' originates from. Word on the street says it was from 'Non-Educated Delinquent'. I'm not convinced and think it was from 'Ne'er do well'.)

Back to the crime of the century...

We gathered round the box while Bill smouldered into the camera with a sideways glance. He informed the nation that the security breach at Haggs Castle was the cunning work of an international gang who knew exactly what they were looking for. Their guile and expertise had outwitted the highly trained staff, with the Wally Dugs obviously stolen to order. They were probably by now nestled in the stash of a collector, or perhaps they had been smuggled abroad. We watched with a mixture of excitement and rage that we'd missed the whole thing!

Just then, one wee girl in the home – she couldn't have been more than 4 years old – sauntered in and stood in front of the telly with her wee pink plastic pram. We were yelling at her...sorry, cajoling her...to get out of the way because we didn't want to miss a second of the action. She just tutted and toddled off, pushing her pram...

...with one of the stolen Wally Dugs neatly wrapped in a blanket!

You could have heard a pin drop. We all stared at each other, clueless as to what to do next. (My complete lack of training left me ill-equipped to deal with such events!)

We called the police. 'Eh, you know that international gang of criminals who out-witted the guards at Haggs Castle...?'

Oh my, how they saw the funny side of it!

Actually, they did. They thought it was hilarious that a 4-year-old and her accomplice had managed to reach up, take those two precious ornaments and walk out with no-one (including us, the staff supposedly in charge) catching them at it.

But the funniest thing was that the other dug – for there were two – had been *'sold'* for sweetie money to another member of our staff who, in an act of kindness, had given the kids a few bob then stuck the dug on top of a wardrobe because it was such an ugly-looking thing!

As far as I can remember no charges were brought, neither against the member of staff nor against the 4-year-old girl.

***

Working in the home during term time was rather odd. For the most part the children were at school, but the staff still had to stick to the set rota, which meant being in a children's home that had no weans.

We could busy ourselves in the morning by taking the children to school to ensure they arrived on time and avoided any 'adventures' en route.

One morning I deposited a 'small boy' (who was 6 inches taller than me) at school assembly, then ran down the corridor secretly delighted that I'd left school behind. (There's something about the smell of a school that can just bring back that sinking feeling in the pit of my stomach. That mix of fear and realisation that either I hadn't done my homework, it was too late to study for the chemistry test, or that I was never going to be asked out by anyone other than the boy who insisted on flicking paper clips at my ear for the best part of four years.) So, there I was skipping down the corridor when that familiar teacher's growl stopped me in my tracks.

'Oi you!' (It was the head teacher.) 'Why are you dressed in those manky jeans? You look a pure state.'

Teachers had a way with words in the 80s!

'Because I'm 22,' I replied, 'and can wear what I like!' (Being petite, I probably did look young for my age.)

His jaw bounced off his knees and he mumbled some sort of apology. As I sauntered off, I realised how childish I still was, because getting 'one over' on a teacher had felt as good as it had when I was at school.

THE GIRL IN THE PICTURE

'You need money and a car, so why not become a Medical Rep?' asked Jess.

'Why don't *you* become a Medical Rep if it's that good?'

'Good God no. I saw enough of them when I was a nurse. Bloody awful job...but I think you'd be good at it,' she added, realising she wasn't exactly selling the idea to me. 'You're a real *people person*, Theresa.'

Jess's assessment of my personality made it sound as though she was a 'donkey person' or a 'sheep person' or such like. Anything but a people person.

'So what'll *you* do?' I asked, assuming that my future was somehow sorted – that all I had to do was saunter in to some drugs company and they'd throw a flash car and pots of money at me.

'Oh, I'm going back to nursing.' She tossed back another margarita without missing a beat. 'I really miss it!'

***

My days as a medical rep are a bit like my days working in the bank – I'd rather not talk about them, but it's my job in a book like this, so I kind of have to!

Despite me being a *'people person'* – whatever the hell

that is – I was a dead loss. To the untrained eye it seemed very glamorous – the aforementioned flash car, good money, conferences abroad… In reality it was crushingly lonely, competitive…and quite aggressive if truth be told.

There were some perks though. Driving about on my own all the time, I soon got to know every cafe and coffee shop in the west of Scotland. And I don't think there was a secondhand shop or antiques market where I didn't know all the staff by name.

There was one fabulous wee place I used to visit in the west end of Glasgow. It restored and sold wooden furniture. The owner was just lovely, a real craftsman who spent time with his customers and never pressured anyone into buying anything. Like me, he was probably a 'people person', which I soon translated into 'crap sales person!' Anyway, in the course of conversation I found out he was a widower and just back from a holiday in Egypt where he had met a wonderful woman from the Lake District. I just love all things Egyptian, and he proceeded to show me his holiday photographs. (These were the days before digital cameras and mobile phones). He pointed out the woman he was smitten with – she too had been on holiday on her own.

'She's beautiful. Are you seeing her again?'

'Oh goodness, I don't think so!'

'Don't tell me you're shy.'

He was indeed shy and really struggled with the idea of contacting this gorgeous woman again, let alone the notion of suggesting a visit.

The following week I went back to the shop. Lo and behold, not only had he called her, but he had actually arranged to visit her for the weekend. Result!

Time passed and I didn't always get a chance to go back into the shop (that's the trouble with work, it can really interrupt your day), and on the days that I did drop by he wasn't there, so I sort of lost touch with his exotic romance. However, a few years later I was driving nearby and thought I'd pop in to see if he was there.

As soon as I stepped inside I recognised a familiar face. It was *her*! Among the wooden furniture stood the gorgeous woman from the holiday pictures. I was absolutely gobsmacked. I asked her if the owner was in.

'Oh my husband's out on a job just now', she replied, 'he'll be back later if you want to come back then.'

Although sorely tempted, I didn't blurt out that I knew her from her picture. I didn't want her to think I was odd. But I was grinning from ear to ear leaving that shop, just thrilled to bits that he'd found the woman of his dreams.

And I never did go back. I wasn't sure if he'd remember me, and perhaps he would think I was some mad stalker if I told him I remembered the minutia of his life. But it still makes me feel warm and happy when I think about it.

THE ROCKY ROAD: FROM CHEMISTS TO SURGERIES TO HOSPITAL WARDS!

Mostly my days as a rep were spent sitting in GP surgeries waiting to see the doctor/practice nurse/practice manager…in fact anyone who would grant me 5 minutes so I could tick the box that said I'd seen someone from that practice. I also had to visit pharmacists in their shops. But instead of me doing the salesperson routine, I usually left laden with things I didn't want: I felt it was rude not to buy anything!

What with the cafes, antique shops and chemists, this job was costing me a fortune, and I soon came to the conclusion that I was no salesperson. Apparently I was the last one in the company to realise this. Just before I plucked up the courage to hand in my resignation, they kindly 'let me go', suggesting that perhaps I would be more suited to 'some other' career! What other career? Was there no end to this hell!?

There I was, almost 30, a string of jobs behind me, and not much in the way of prospects. My skill base was limited, and my hobbies – tap dancing, singing, eating and writing – didn't transfer well into the jobs market. Yes, I'd written stories and articles (all unpublished) since my teens, but being a writer wasn't really a proper job. No-one made a living out of being a writer. Well, no-one

I knew anyway.

So I decided to do some voluntary work while I filled out application upon application for some jobs I didn't want or indeed get. And so I think it must have been fate that landed me at the doors of Hairmyres Hospital in East Kilbride as a volunteer with their radio station.

There were a smattering of older people on board, but it seemed to be mainly teenage boys on the rota. They looked at me as though I was ancient. I suppose to them a 30-year-old woman *was* ancient.

What struck me most about Hospital Radio was how professional and well-run it was. This was no Mickey Mouse operation. No Amateur Hour hokey set-up. No Siree. This was the real deal, crammed with radio anoraks determined to broadcast the best possible programmes to the patients of Hairmyres. (Being a radio anorak myself I can use that term with affection, and the confidence of knowing it's actually a compliment to those in the know!)

First job: going round the wards visiting patients, having a chat and taking requests. I was taken aback at how vital hospital radio stations are to patients. I just hadn't realised. Many people are in long-term and their days can stretch on forever; some are far from home so visits from family and friends are sporadic; and of course in some cases people have very few – or sometimes *no* – visitors at all.

As volunteers we did the ward rounds 2 or 3 times a week, and it's amazing how much we looked forward to it.

(It's tempting to say 'them' when talking about patients, but it should really be 'us'. None of us know when we may end up in hospital for whatever reason. In fact one volunteer was struck by appendicitis and woke from the anaesthetic to find me shoving a piece of paper under his nose asking, 'Would you like us to play you a wee song, Alan?')

If anyone is looking for a career in radio I suggest they start with Hospital Radio. It'll soon let them know what's involved and help determine if they really are interested in broadcasting or not. To be honest, I don't meet many people who are interested in radio – it's mostly television people are seduced by. Or rather, the chance to be famous.

I meet numerous trainees/work placement scheme personnel (again I think they're called 'service users' but we just call them 'people') who all want to work 'on telly' and our conversations usually go like this...

ME: What is it you'd like to do?
THEM: Work in the media.
ME: Doing what?
THEM: Just anything.
ME: What? Desktop publishing?

I usually get a blank look with this one.

THEM: No, telly.

ME: Doing what?

I find the broken-record technique works – keep asking the same question until you get an answer. On 'telly' it's called a Paxman!

THEM: Anything.

This answer is usually a lie, which I can prove with the following line of enquiry.

ME: What, like driving the Sat Truck? Organising location shots? Catering for outside broadcasts?
THEM: No, you know, presenting like.
ME: Oh right, what kind of programmes?
THEM: Just anything.

After that I repeat stage 4 of the questioning, replacing the various jobs with a diverse range of programmes such as *University Challenge*, *The Sky at Night*, *One Man and his Dog*, *Strictly Come Dancing*...ad infinitum until they get bored and walk away.

Anyway, where was I? Oh yes, hospital radio.
   So, within weeks of volunteering, when I wasn't visiting the wards, I was playing around with the equipment – finding out how things worked, learning how to edit on

tape. This was back in the day of the razor blade, a china pencil and sticky tape. Strangely I found that addictive – therapeutic almost.

There were always other volunteers on hand who were willing to spend time and teach you what you needed to know. It was easy to pick out the ones who were genuinely interested in creating the best possible sound and who wanted to hone their craft. And it's great to see their hard work and dedication has paid off, as many of the youngsters went on to forge a career in broadcasting, especially Alan Shaw (he of the appendicitis fame).

Alan was only 17 when we met and he went out of his way to show me the ropes. It's great to see him now as one of the key players at West FM. He genuinely is one of the nicest men working in radio today. Well, I say 'men'…he still looks exactly the same as when he was a teenager. He must have a picture rotting away in the attic somewhere!

I know this sounds a bit naff, but I do owe them all a debt of gratitude; they were really kind and helpful and tolerant. I also learned a lot from the patients I visited each week. Everyone had a unique story to tell; and although I initially went along as a volunteer to 'help' in whatever way I could, I came away with a real sense of having made a difference. In a way, the patients helped *me* as much as I helped them.

Bear in mind I was considered quite old to be changing horses mid-stream and embarking on a radio career. But, when I did, my time at Hairmyres meant I had a very credible set of skills under my belt. I could interview, produce, edit, sound-check a studio, actually operate a studio…and of course talk out loud on the wireless, which is what I continue to do.

AYE WRITE!

They say if you find a job you like, then you'll never truly work again. And I have to say it's true. For all the early mornings and night shifts, for all the standing in the cold and/or rain waiting for an exclusive interview, and even for the stress of a big hairy editor yelling that you've got 3 minutes to meet your deadline or you're out on your ear, a career in radio certainly beats working for a living!

Yes I know it's work, and it's often *hard* work with long hours, *and* it's increasingly competitive. But it doesn't *feel* like work and that's what counts.

Right, so there I was, a volunteer at Hairmyres Hospital and loving every minute of it, but volunteering doesn't pay the rent. I was married at the time and my long-suffering husband promised he wouldn't let me starve, but I had to face it: I needed a job. A proper job. I was still doing part-time or temporary bits and pieces here and there, but I really was getting a bit long in the tooth to be a Pepsi Challenge Girl.

It was around this time that I thought perhaps I should, after all, try my hand at being a writer.

I'd like to blame my mother for all this nonsense. I know it's commonplace to lay the blame for all our mistakes at our parents' feet, but Mum encouraged me in all my pursuits. To most, such encouragement won't sound like a bad thing, but if I'd said I wanted to be an astronaut she would have phoned NASA and demanded that they interview me.

Mum also let me go to school with calypso sleeves pinned to my standard-issue grey jersey, which gave me a misguided sense that everything I did was normal – no matter how whacky it seemed to others. For those of you who don't know what calypso sleeves are (and why should you?!), they're a sort of multi-coloured, multi-layered sleeve favoured by calypso performers. They were popular in the 1950s, but this was 1970s Glasgow. *The X Factor* hadn't been invented and 10-year-olds were all relatively normal. They played with bikes and didn't feel the need to dress up as Carmen Miranda!

So, calypso sleeves a distant memory, and with my grown-up head on, I bought a secondhand typewriter (this was *way* before the days of computers) and settled down to write a masterpiece.

I sat and stared out of the window for days. It was less painful than staring at the blank piece of paper that was giving me snow blindness.

There's nothing else I can say on this matter. Case closed.

IS THIS THE RIGHT BUS
FOR THE BBC?

Much as I loved Hospital Radio, at the time I still didn't realise that I could actually have a career in 'real' radio. Where would I start? What would I do? How would I let those in charge of Radioland know what I was capable of?

A tremendous amount of luck was involved in what happened next.

There's an old saying: 'The harder I work the luckier I seem to get'. Who said this first is anyone's guess – it's been attributed to Samuel Goldwyn, Gary Player, Arnold Palmer and even Norman Wisdom! And yes, nothing replaces hard work in any career, but you need a few lucky breaks too.

One day, on the way into Glasgow on the bus – the 66 if you're into detail – I overheard a conversation. (I can't stop eavesdropping; other folk's chat always seems more interesting!) Someone was talking about a course at the BBC for unemployed people. That was all the information I got… oh, apart from the immortal line, 'Ah'm no goin' oot wae him – he's gote a moustache'.

This second snippet of information was infinitely funnier than the first but served me little use in securing gainful employment (although if I ever do write a play, be sure that very line will be shoe-horned in somewhere). A course at the BBC, on the other hand, was a whole different ball-game. It could be right up my street.

I was a regular at the Job Centre by now and, short of going on their Christmas night out, felt I was almost part of the team. So I nipped in to ask about this wonderful training course where media wannabes like myself could forge ahead with their chosen career.

Alas, no-one knew what I was talking about. To be fair, relating an overheard conversation on the No. 66 probably didn't count as giving them much to go on, but I did a bit of digging myself and pestered the Job Centre peeps to keep hunting for the elusive course. And eventually I found that, yes, there was indeed a 'media skills' course based at the BBC in Glasgow.

E Force was a European initiative with government funding to help the long-term unemployed. (I later discovered the 'E' stood for 'European' – yes, that was rather lost on me too!). Fortuitously, they were holding interviews that very month for the autumn influx of 'students'. (At this point I feared I was destined to be a student until the end of my days.)

The interview must have gone well, because before I knew it I had a start date and a timetable and a new pen and a ring-bind folder…everything.

During the first day we were asked what area of study we preferred – radio or desktop publishing. (That's why I always ask *that question* to folk who tell me they want to work in the media.) Desktop publishing, I thought? No thank you! I hadn't a clue what it even was, but I was surprised at the number of people who opted for it. I thought *everyone* just wanted to work in radio!

The course lasted a year and fine-tuned everything I thought I'd already learned at Hospital Radio. In addition, we were taught broadcasting libel law and the legal aspects of journalism.

I'll never forget a field trip to Radio Clyde to have a look around their studios and newsroom. The MD at the time told us he'd proudly announced to a media lawyer that he insisted all his presenters used a 6-second delay during live broadcasts – to ensure there would never be a problem with libellous output. Apparently the lawyer nodded sagely and said, 'Really? It can take a high court judge and a string of barristers anything up to a year to settle a libel case. You think your DJs can make that call in 6 seconds!'

TESTING...TESTING...IS THIS THING SWITCHED ON?

At the end of the BBC Training Course we had to undertake up to 4 weeks' practical work experience. It was up to each student to seek out a suitable placement. The lecturers would then endeavour to help us in our quest.

I decided a stint as a traffic reporter at AA Roadwatch was a good option. I knew that, had I opted for a radio station, I would have had little chance of actually broadcasting. But at Roadwatch *everyone* was a broadcaster, so I reckoned I had a good chance of getting 'on-air' whilst still a trainee.

Thankfully my hunch paid off. Also thankfully, it was in the summer and there was a lot of holiday cover to fill, so after a couple of weeks shadowing the established team members I was let loose to fly solo.

I'll never forget my first time on live, proper, grown-up radio. My heart was beating so loud that I could hear it pounding in my ears. And I was convinced everyone else could hear it too. Suffice to say I made my usual gaff of speaking far too quickly, with the result that no-one could understand a word. But at least I got it over with rapidly!

Once I'd learned to slow down – I still speak far too quickly actually – I began to feel more comfortable on air, and although I was always just that wee bit nervous, the

47

blood rushing through my ears stopped sounding like a freight train and calmed to a gentle whirring that was just enough to remind me that my nerves were lurking in the background.

***

The shift pattern was fairly gruelling. Split shifts started at 5am, finished before lunchtime then saw us back in for the afternoon slot from 3–7pm. Needless to say, if you were on a split shift you only got paid for the hours worked, and all for an hourly rate of just a few pence above the minimum wage.

As freelancers we could work as little or as much as we liked, but it was very much frowned upon if you turned down a shift. And if you hacked off the person doing the rota you could be guaranteed early shift both Saturdays and Sundays until you either bought them breakfast at the canteen or brought in some biscuits as a peace offering.

We're a petty bunch in radio!

Often we worked 7 days on the trot (early or late or sometimes both) then had one day off before being back on another 7-day shift pattern. But there were times when some of us worked 21 days in a row. (EU directives about working hours and staff contracts were yet to be invented.)

Most of Scotland's radio stations subscribed to the AA for their travel updates. So, on any one shift you could be broadcasting on Radios Tay, Forth and Clyde as well as owner's sister (in more ways than one) and was just enjoying a wee break.

Once I was sure the property was free from rising damp, deathwatch beetle and religious personnel, I made sure it was mine.

***

Now all I had to do was footer about, employing Mum's tried and trusted method for gardening – chatting to a few neighbours, dishing out the odd cuppa – and my green-fingered genius would reveal itself to all and sundry.

Within a year the Nun was gone (she actually left before I moved in) and the lush green lawn had developed male pattern baldness. In year two the fruit trees developed some sort of black rot and the hollyhocks hung heavy with rust. Indeed, within three years (I swear it was just the blink of an eye) the garden turned on me. There's no other way to describe it. It became a thicket of brambles and thorns and weird scratchy stingy things that stuck to my clothes and snapped at the back door like a hungry wolf.

Dad would visit often, look out at this now jungle while lighting his pipe and offer some pearls of wisdom. 'Would you not prefer to live in a nice flat?' was his verbal weapon of choice, from which I was to gleam that the garden was out of control. 'Hah!' I'd reply, gesticulating outside to the now crumbling stairways, cracked paths and snarling monstrous weeds. 'And give all this up!?'

Then he would take off his jacket, clearly defeated, and say, 'Where is it?'

'Where's what?' I'd say, knowing full well what he meant.

'That thing,' he'd say, moving his hands back and forth by way of explanation, in the way that he did when he couldn't remember the name of something. 'You know, the thing like a hoover which mows the lawn'.

'Oh the lawn-mower?' I'd say.

'Yes' he'd say.

And I would tip my chin towards the shed and hope I looked as innocent and saintly as Sister Eleanora.

And so it came to pass that for many years we employed that routine. It became our method of maintaining that piece of land. I daren't call it gardening. I just daren't.

Scot FM.

The set-up was the strangest thing, when I think back. It was a long narrow room at the headquarters in Erskine. One side was a huge internal window that looked out onto the call centre, and behind the glass were the 'broadcasters'. The room was split into booths, each with its own tiny self-contained studio.

Because we were broadcasting on several stations at once, we had to 'line-up' with the correct station before each bulletin. That meant running to the end of the room, pulling a jack-ended wire from a huge box that looked like an old telephone exchange, and plugging it onto the next station. But it meant us all having to work like clockwork; if you 'pulled the plug' before an announcer had finished his or her bulletin you quite literally cut them off in their prime. So my stint at Roadwatch provided ideal training in 'timing' – training I've clung to throughout my career in radio.

PASSING WATER AND
TAMING THE TIGER...

It's worth me explaining the difference between 'traffic' and 'travel' in the context of radio broadcasting, because the terms are used interchangeably by listeners but have specific meanings to those of us in Radioland. Put simply: 'traffic' is the system whereby audio is sent to and from different stations; whereas 'travel' is...well, it's what I do!

Travel reporters do all their own check calls and write all their own scripts. We collate the information from a variety of sources: the police are the first port of call (we do check calls at least every hour); then we're in touch with organisations such as Scotrail, the fire service (Scottish Fire & Rescue to give them their proper name), Traffic Scotland, local councils...in fact anyone who has travel information.

Back in my AA Roadwatch days we even called local garages and shops that were on main roads so we could get a good 'look' as the rush hour unfolded. And of course each week we received (faxed at that time) huge lists of proposed roadworks for the entire country. It was some poor soul's job to make sure each and every one was up-to-date and handwritten into the database. Again, giving the person in charge a decent packet of biscuits, or an impromptu roll & sausage from the canteen, could get you off the hook and ensure the task would be given to someone less well versed in the all-important black art of office politics.

However, the most vital information came from the listeners. We gave the number out as often as possible to encourage people to keep in touch. It was especially important in those days before social media and networking sites.

Listener information is still essential today, though sometimes listeners don't seem to realise it. Often when people call the first thing they say is, 'I'm sorry to bother you, but...' They have no idea how much we need their call.

The rest of the sentence is usually along the lines of, '...can you tell that girl who does the travel there's a breakdown/accident/traffic jam at...'

Nine times out of ten they're surprised when I tell them, 'I *am* that girl'.

'Oh, d'you not have an assistant to answer your phone?' they'll then ask, clearly upset that we run such a two-bit operation.

Back in the day, the job was like a juggling act: trying to write a legible script (they were all hand-written), making sure you stuck to your allocated time, doing the pushy-pully thing with the wires and sockets, doing the check calls, answering the phones and just generally trying to sound jolly... It was all an invaluable start to a career in broadcasting.

There was some great banter too. And a fair few gaffs.

I still cringe at the thought of my first broadcasts during the bad storms, when rivers burst their banks and there was a lot of localised flooding. In an instant I gained notoriety as the woman who said in her poshest radio voice, 'And remember, drivers, if you need to pass water today make sure you take great care.' The next day that quote was in Tom Shields Diary page in what was then the *Glasgow Herald*.

Although we spoke every day to the presenters of whatever radio stations we were broadcasting on, we never actually met them face to face. And, as you can imagine, most of the best chat was 'off-air' in the few seconds we had before the bulletins. Weekends were always less manic, giving us more time to converse.

Some presenters were more chatty than others. And one who could talk for Scotland was 'Tiger' Tim Stevens. Tim was a stalwart on Clyde 1 and a bit of a legend. His trademark was a big Tiger Suit – a sort of furry onesie that he wore well before they ever became fashionable. Tim always liked to give his listeners a bit of chat – he was well known for his cheek but ended each programme with a sincere "God Bless and Goodbye", urging each and every one of us to take care and be nice to one and other. The usual stuff.

Anyway, chatting away one day I told him a really

cheesy expression that I thought would go down well: *'Remember, a stranger is just a friend you do not know yet'*. There's an old song with that line. (The song truly is awful, but Tim thought it'd be a great way to end his show.) Now, I know I'm prone to exaggerating, but I honestly fed Tim that line at least 20 times...and he still couldn't get it right. We went over it and over it before he was due to go on air to finish his programme, but he kept getting it wrong.

'Oh for goodness sake, Tim, write the bloody thing down, it's only 10 words.'

'Aye, aye, I'll get it right, don't worry,' he assured me.

By this time I was bent double with laughter at his appalling attempts to make this corny script sound sincere. 'A stranger is just...what was it again?'

This seemed to go on for an eternity before he was about to go back on-air and say it live to an audience. The final bed of music to close his show began to play and Tim lowered his voice to his caring, sharing, sincere whisper, making sure we all knew he was talking to us and us alone. And then he came in with his new killer line... 'Goodbye, God Bless and remember...a stranger's a person you do not know.'

GOING BANANAS IN PYJAMAS WITH THE ONE-LEGGED GOALKEEPER

From AA Roadwatch I was 'invited' to work as a news journalist at Q96, a wee commercial radio station in Paisley. Sadly it no longer exists, but I can honestly say the funniest times of my career were spent there.

I was living in Paisley at the time (which I'd forgotten until I wrote this!) so it was only a hop, skip and a jump away. There was a cross-over period during which I did my Roadwatch shifts mid-week then read the news at Q96 every Saturday.

The station had seen better days, if truth be told. It was housed in a dingy converted factory in Lady Lane. Lady Lane sounds rather posh; it wasn't. But I didn't care. I was working for a real radio station and I was in my element!

On my first morning at Q my alarm clock failed to go off: in other words, I slept in, something I've only done twice in my career. I awoke at 6.30 and was supposed to be reading the 7am news. I had no option but to run out the door in my pyjamas, grabbing last night's clothes on the way.

I'm not sure if turning up on my first day in my jammies made a terribly good impression, but once again my unique selling points (I was cheap and available) rose to the fore and they kept me on.

After that, it was a common occurrence for me to wear my jammies to work. There's a strange bonding process that takes place during early shifts on radio. Any tiny little scrap of advice that can guarantee an extra 10 minutes in bed is valued currency and devoured by colleagues. Strangely, none of them picked up on the night-clothes technique; they all appeared each day fully clothed.

You can probably gather it wasn't the most disciplined of working environments. Every day around lunchtime, I would get dressed (I didn't wear my jammies for the whole shift!) and I'd nip to the pub next door with the sales team. (I want to add here that the money was appalling in case you're thinking I was getting paid to drink away my afternoons.)

The pub (The Cellar if you're interested) provided the excellent service of playing Q through the speakers. That way I could listen out for the last song before the news and then sprint as fast as my legs would carry me back into the studio to read the bulletin. For a while my 'breathy' delivery was my trademark! Then I'd be back to the pub for lunch and wine and chat. It's amazing how those three things can make an afternoon disappear.

They were great days. I was bad, but the sales team was much worse. It wasn't unheard of for them to saunter off to the pictures, or take a wee trip to the coast for the afternoon. They didn't have the constraints of having to be behind a mic every hour on the hour.

***

As with most of the broadcasting media across the world, Saturdays were devoted to sport. Well football really. And at one point we were lucky enough to have Ally McLeod as a regular pundit.

For those of you too young to remember, Ally was the Scotland Manager for a time. He and his Tartan Army promised to win the World Cup in Argentina in 1978. And we had no reason not to believe this. But, it all went horribly wrong and the crestfallen Ally and the Scotland Squad came home with hardly a pot to p*ss in never mind a trophy.

I felt really sorry for him at the time, but when he came through the doors of Lady Lane all that unpleasant business was well behind him. Every Saturday he would turn up as cheery as a cheery thing and do his stint on-air. He was such a likeable man. Really funny and self-effacing, he hated missing out on any chat or office gossip.

Ally started his career as a professional footballer in 1949, when the world was a very different place. He had me in stitches when he told me about travelling to Germany and being 'led into a topless bar'. He said the sight of all those naked breasts almost brought him to a point of collapse, and he was sure he was going to go blind! This was at a time when the women in Glasgow still wore

headscarves and kept their hands on their ha'pennies!²*
He was mortified and had to beg his teammates not to tell
his Mammy where he'd been.

Ally came from a footballing family and I also recall
him swearing blind that his dad (or it may have been his
grandfather) had been a goalkeeper. That in itself wouldn't
be strange. What *was* strange was that the man only had
one leg! And was so casual was he that he used to prop
his wooden leg against the goalpost and try make heroic
one-legged 'saves' to show off. Alas I fear his career was
short lived!

---

2 * In the days before tights – when a glimpse of stocking was considered shocking
– women often used small coins as a makeshift repair if the fastener came off
their suspenders. The advice – passed on from mothers to daughters going out on
dates – was always to 'keep your hand on yer ha'penny' to ensuring that no arduous
suitor could force his hand up the girl's skirt. Birth control was very simple in the
60s!!

IS THERE ANYBODY THERE...?

During my time at Q, I[3]* was promoted to News Editor. That just meant I was in charge of the rotas, but it looked good on my CV. Perhaps this promotion went to my head, because I soon fancied trying my hand at presenting. Newsreaders are always trying to 'big up' their part.

I bent a few ears and was given a chance to host...wait for it...the Psychic Phone In!!

Perhaps I should have read the warning signs of what was to follow. And please, no jokes along the lines of 'you should have seen it coming'.

The station had a resident clairvoyant with his own Saturday-night phone-in during which he would 'connect with the other side'. The programme had a rather strange format: the presenter would play a tune, give a bit of chat, then introduce Derek The Psychic and invite people to call. Derek would then try to relay a message from the caller's loved ones...which usually involved telling them they had a leaky washing machine.

It was the most popular show at the station. I had no idea so many people were desperate to talk to their dead relatives. Because of some guideline or other (and it was the first time we'd ever adhered to anything resembling

---

3   * Were it not for my pesky editor inserting the comma in this sentence, you could have been (wrongly) impressed that I'd worked with Stephen Fry!

a guideline) callers had to start each conversation with, 'Have you got a message for me, Derek?'

(I always thought 'Derek' a rather unassuming name for a psychic and tried to convince him to change it to Dirk. My advice fell on deaf ears.)

This was my big chance to wow everyone with my presenting skills. I even got to pick the opening tune. I remember it so well: Andy Williams (more of him later) singing *The House of Bamboo*. It's an upbeat number with bongo drums and probably wasn't in keeping with the sombre tone of the programme, but what did I know about playlists?

Derek the Psychic was not amused...and I'm afraid it went downhill after that.

The first caller came through, but someone had 'switched' the lines in the main studio. So, although I could hear them, they couldn't hear me. I tweaked a few knobs and pressed some buttons until finally...they could hear me but I couldn't hear them!

It was time to implement the emergency guidelines. I followed them to the letter, i.e. I frantically pressed every button on the desk until one worked. Only this time *none* did.

Twenty minutes later, we were still yelling down the phone, pressing buttons and pushing faders, all in a desperate bid to get our callers 'live on air' so they could talk to dead people.

And all this was being broadcast. Every single

cringeworthy minute of it. I just kept playing more and more music…except that it wasn't more and more, it was the same tune over and over – I only had one record with me! There were CDs close by, but I was in such a flap that I didn't have time to even take them off the shelf!

And, because of the set-up of that particular studio, I couldn't play music *and* test the phone lines at the same time. So I would mute the music every few minutes, but every time I did we'd get a golden on-air nugget such as, 'This is shite…that lassie cannae hear me,' followed by the bored caller slamming their phone down.

By this time Derek was livid and refused to go on air. He claimed I had sucked all the psychic energy out of him, but I was pretty sure that wasn't a sackable offence, so I told him to pull himself together and just carry on.

However, he was having none of it and went into the office to phone his mum.

Mrs Derek must have talked some sense into him because he marched back in to the studio with his arms folded tightly across his chest and a smug look that told me I wasn't worth bothering about.

Eventually – the programme was 3 hours long so there was no escape – we managed to get the studio up and running. Hooray! Eventually we managed to get a caller on-air. Yippee! And eventually I could stop playing *House of Bamboo*, which by this time was on a loop – in my head as much as on the radio!

As it transpired, I rather enjoyed the rest of the

programme. But apparently I didn't quite 'get it'. You see, when callers started telling Derek The Psychic their problems, and while he was looking to the other side for answers, I would butt in with my own 'helpful' home-spun advice. The show disintegrated into mayhem…

And Derek never forgave me. He refused to work with me ever again and said I was hopeless. I was taken off the programme. In truth I'm sure it was because I refused to run him home afterwards and he took the hump at having to fork out for a taxi.

But it all ended well. Derek went on to become quite famous and had his own TV show. And ironically I got a taste for the spirit world (and no, I don't mean the '40% Vol' kind) and have been a keen follower ever since!

***

Technical mishaps aside, we were all one big happy Q96 family. The managing director, the sales team, the journalists, the DJs and Agnes the cleaner…we all just sort of mucked in and made sure the station had its own unique style.

It was the sort of place at which the aforementioned Agnes would sometimes read out the weather for us, infusing her performances with a special kind of dead-pan delivery that no-one else could match.

The very same Agnes also turned polishing into an art form. Her pride and joy was the cheese plant that stood in the main corridor. She spent hours rubbing the huge leaves with a soft cloth, at the same time imparting her sage-like wisdom to anyone who passed by. And her passers-by included Adam Faith, Right Said Fred and no lesser stars than The Crankies!

Actually, looking back it's hardly surprising the place closed down; we existed in a sort of broadcasting bubble, and somehow muddled through. In truth, much of what happened at Q – in fact much of what's happened at many radio stations I've worked at – can't be printed for reasons of privacy...and so I don't get sued.

The Q96 building may have been run-down, and its equipment may all have been rather tired, with the plastic chairs and mismatched office furniture in stark contrast to the slickness of the BBC, but we had some laughs, played some music and could boast Radioland's most polished cheese plant.

THEY SAY SHE TOUCHED A NATION...

One morning during the wee small hours the phone rang. This was nothing new – it's what phones do. I was working for Radio Clyde at the time and often got calls to come in to the station at short notice if there was a breaking story, or even if another reporter had called in sick. It was the last Sunday of August, 1997 – August the 31st – and my news editor was on the other end of the line. My first thought was *how the hell can I get out of going into work today?'* My brain scrambled for every possible excuse.

'Princess Diana's been in a car crash,' were the first words he said to me. My ears immediately pricked up and I forced myself awake. '...She was in Paris and by all accounts was travelling along with Dodi Fayed when the accident happened. He's died at the scene.'

There was no doubt this was a story. A *big* story. But it still didn't make sense. How could I possibly cover the story from Glasgow? Every news agency in the world would have its own Parisian correspondents and would be filing copy and sound bites to all the main stations.

My Editor seemed to be dragging the words out and took what appeared to be an age to actually tell me what had happened.

'...She [Diana] suffered a heart attack as a result of her injuries...she died on the operating table.'

I couldn't really take in what I was hearing. People like Princess Diana did not die. And certainly not in car smashes in Parisian Tunnels.

This was in the days before rolling news programmes were commonplace. *BBC News 24* was in its infancy and, like its commercial rival, Sky, was only available on digital. And the information super-highway was not what we know today. Twitter and Facebook hadn't even been invented – the internet was still a relatively new development. And few people had mobile phones, let alone smartphones. Access to information was very limited.

I flicked on both the television and radio to see if I could get any more information as I threw on some clothes. My staff taxi beeped its horn before I could tune into anything relevant and I ran out the door.

It was all hands to the pumps. Princess Diana was the most loved member of the British Royal Family, so this was the biggest story of the century. When I arrived at Radio Clyde the newsroom was going like a fair. Every reporter had been called in, along with the Editors and the Managing Director.

The 'wires' were working overtime, with updates streaming through every few seconds. Each new piece of copy or audio needed to be edited and downloaded onto a format we could play in the news bulletins. There were interviews from local police, politicians, doctors on the scene…in fact anyone who would speak was interviewed, and of course there were seemingly endless vox-pops of locals in Paris who now claimed to have eye-witness accounts. Within an hour of the story breaking there must have been three hundred people who claimed to have seen Diana and Dodi in their final hour together, or who had watched the Mercedes disappear into the Pont De l'Alma road tunnel, never to come out the other side.

It was easy to tell the genuine eye-witnesses from the glory hunters, but in the first couple of hours every single piece of audio had to be recorded.

We were each assigned a job spec. I was told to take the Clyde Jeep out into Glasgow city centre to speak to as many 'ordinary punters' as I could. We needed to know the public's reaction to this appalling news.

It was still only 7am, *and* it was a Sunday, so the only place I could find any signs of life was Buchanan Street Bus Station, where I caught passengers getting off the sleeper services from Manchester and London.

It's hard to believe that each and every person I spoke to was completely oblivious to the tragedy. I didn't have my press-pass with me (such was the rush) and some actually thought I was playing a sick joke and refused to speak to me. Like the rest of the world they were in a state of shock at the news.

By the time I ran back to the station to get the audio edited and ready for broadcast it was 9am and news of Diana's death was filtering through to every household in the country.

I knew this was unfolding into one of the biggest stories of the century, but I had no idea of the outpouring of public grief that was to follow.

By the time I made my second trip into Glasgow city centre, George Square was a sea of colour. Floral tributes carpeted the entire area. There was nothing official at this point, but Glasgow's public needed somewhere to pay their respects.

I'm not ashamed to say I was really shocked at the tidal wave of grief Diana's death had created. I'm not sure what the reason was for it. Yes she was 'loved' in that way adoring fans love their idols, but this was something quite unprecedented. People were sobbing as they laid flowers, photographs, messages. I spoke to one woman who actually said the death of Diana was worse than losing her own mother! I really wasn't prepared for this. I had no idea Diana held such a dear place in her public's heart. Indeed, even now I'm not convinced that she did. Perhaps there was something else going on that none of us could put a finger on, perhaps we needed a focus for our collective emotions in an age where death is a taboo subject and our grief factored out to counsellors and help-lines, because the outpouring came even from people who in normal circumstances wouldn't think twice about behaving in this way over the death of a royal – or former royal.

The City Chambers opened a book of remembrance

for the Princess and within seconds there was a queue four deep around the entire block of the building. Again, men, women and children wept openly as they waited to pay their respects. One young man, probably in his late twenties, was sobbing inconsolably; his girlfriend's arm around his shoulder was doing little to comfort him.

I was invited to sign the book, and if my memory serves me correctly, mine was either the first or second signature on the opening page. I felt such a fraud; behind me people were beside themselves with grief, and although I was shocked and certainly very saddened by the death of this young woman – this mother who had left behind two young boys ill-prepared to face the world – I honestly couldn't conjure the collective grief that was palpable around me. I can't even remember what I wrote. Something very simple like, *Diana, Rest In Peace.* I just couldn't think of anything else to say. And, as I turned and saw the genuine sorrow weaving its way through the queue of mourners, I knew there would be a backlash. Someone would have to pay for this, be it the press, the Royal Household, or whoever; Diana's death would have long-lasting consequences.

***

Within a day, the very same mourners who had gladly chatted to the press about their loss were shouting abuse at journalists in the street, accusing each and every one of us of contributing to that fatal car crash.

I recall a particular incident when I parked my Clyde Jeep (very visible with its bright-red paint job and distinctive white lettering) to go and do an interview in the outskirts of Glasgow. I passed about a dozen or so people who were obviously chatting about the tragedy. Most were carrying newspapers featuring pictures of Diana and with details about the accident filling every available column inch. As soon as they saw me they let rip. 'Vulture!' someone shouted. I looked around, trying to see who this dreadful beast was. It was me! 'Can you not let her rest in peace?' asked another. And then came, 'Your f*cking mob drove her to her death.' After which the insults came thick and fast.

I was absolutely dumbfounded at the sheer venom directed toward me. It wasn't me personally, I understood (nearly). It was journalists in general.

As is my want, I tried to reason with them. Even saying 'them' is rather alien to me and suggests that as a journalist I was already divided from members of the public – from the listeners. But nothing could be further from the truth. I too was a listener, a viewer and a reader.

As I said, almost all of the small gathering were holding newspapers, desperate to devour every last morsel of information about Diana. I explained that it was the world's desire for information on Diana that had led the press to pursue her every move. A publication with the Princess's picture on the front cover was guaranteed a doubling of sales.

Grief is a terrible thing and it robs most of us of the sense to think straight. Every newspaper and magazine in the country was instantly devoted to the aftermath of that now infamous Parisian Car Crash. And each edition sold out as fast as it hit the shops. The hunger for information on Diana was as potent as ever, and each and every news agency responded to this desire by churning out more and more. And yet still the press, as though it were an independent beast acting outwith the laws of supply and demand, was blamed for hounding Diana to her death. Mob rule, it would appear, is the most dangerous beast of all.

TEA AND GREEN FINGERS

Gardening was always seen as a slightly 'strange' pass-time in our house – a hobby for middle-class couples with too much time on their hands...and nae weans. Dad was a master cabinet-maker. A craftsman who could fashion even the most basic bits of wood into something wonderful, he viewed the lawnmower with healthy suspicion; a dangerous contraption designed to rob him of hours he wanted to spend on more artistic pursuits. Our mum on the other hand *talked* a good game, and regaled us with stories of her own father, who was the first person in the world to cultivate a black tulip. To this day we don't know if that is true, as he died in 1932 and took his gardening skills with him. Whatever, it gave Mum the edge in the horticultural department and she was considered the expert, the green-fingered one of the operation.

Dad was relieved of grass-cutting duties forever when we moved to a main door tenement flat. We had a small double-fronted garden. It looked onto the street and certainly wasn't big enough for a lawn. For most families with 4 children that might have been a problem, but for my dad that feature alone clinched the deal. And so it was there, in that plot the size of a postage stamp, that Mum would spend many hours footering about to her heart's content. In truth, she didn't do a lot of 'gardening' as such, it was more random seed sowing and hacking down occasional wayward shrubs.

No, for Mum the pursuit of the soil meant going out at whatever time she was free – usually 10pm, the street-light illuminating her tasks – and stopping for a chat with anyone who passed by. Since we were on one of the main streets in the area, she soon attracted a healthy crowd after 'closing time'. And it was here Mum held court, often chatting into the wee small hours.

Despite the lack of green-fingered activity, our garden developed into a sort of Mecca for anyone who fancied some company. Copious amounts of tea was handed out on those late summer evenings, along with friendly words of wisdom. (There was never any alcohol; I grew up in a tea-total house and even coffee was regarded as rather exotic.) Great wrongs were put to right, broken hearts mended and friendships forged. But most of all we had a laugh.

As far as I can remember the only thing of note that actually grew in that garden was an Acer Palmatum; a Japanese Maple. Mum would point and claim she had it imported from Japan at great expense, and it *was* very unusual to see one growing in Glasgow! But in truth it had been there before we moved in, and Mum always made sure only to make her claim to those who were either ignorant of, or uninterested in, all things horticultural.

On occasion the night-time gardening would take

on a strange twist. A few times a year the local butcher would have 'big orders' to prepare, especially at Easter and Christmas (gardening in our house was never the seasonal activity it should have been), and the master butcher and his boys would often work through the night to make sure everything was ready in time. It was on those night's that Mum's garden party became a moveable feast, and she would make huge ashets of homemade chips to take down to the boys in the shop. No-one ever thought it was an unusual sight for my Mum to wander down the street at some ridiculous hour, carrying a tray of piping hot chips, the salty steam wafting the delicious aroma for miles around. She could always recruit a helper to assist in the carrying, then she'd beat a hasty retreat to the garden in case she missed any gossip.

Probably very few horticultural skills were passed on to me during this time, and to be honest the garden never really looked any different from one year to the next. Instead, what it did do was instil a love of being outdoors in my own wee green space, and the sense that gardening is about more than making things grow. It's about love and passion and humour and community and sharing; most of all sharing. The most beautiful garden in the world is a barren landscape if you don't allow others to share it.

NUN LOVED GARDENING MORE THAN I!

When I finally got my own garden many years later I was in for a bit of a shock...

I'll never forget going to see the house for the first time. A semi-detached stone-built cottage on the outskirts of Glasgow. Charming enough from the street; a small front lawn, a few flower beds and even the ubiquitous roses growing round the door.

So far so good.

Inside, the house itself was standard fare really, nothing to make it stand out from the crowd. But when I was ushered through to the back of the property I became totally spellbound. For tucked away out of sight from the street was *the* most fabulous secret garden, bursting with colour and scent. A real assault on the senses. The owner invited me to explore.

I picked my way through the sloping terraces, the winding path over-spilling with lavender, hollyhocks and peony roses. Overhead, fruit trees groaned with apples and pears. Each twist, each turn offered another hidden gem. I ventured down the makeshift rickety stairway, my heart fluttering with excitement as I carefully parted the tall grasses that led to a hidden, sunken lawn. Would this reveal some more treasure? A fabulous rare orchid? An undiscovered gem?

I held my breath as pin pricks of inky blackness dappled into view. Surely not the elusive black tulip! Dear Mother of God, perhaps a whole bed of them. I waited just a few seconds, faltering before I pulled back the curtain of weeping willow to get a better look. And there it was. Slap bang in the middle of the back-green, the only monochrome item in the entire landscape. A...nun.

I pushed all thoughts of *The Sound of Music* to the back of my brain and regained my composure!

Reclining on a swing chair with a fringed canopy, she looked quite at home in this little oasis. This was almost a better find than the black tulip. I was tempted to say, 'Dr Livingston, I presume,' so shocked was I at the sight of her. Only her face was visible beneath her gown and wimple and she tipped her chin by way of hello when she saw me. Then went back to swinging her legs and smiling up at the sun.

I had this notion that Sister Eleanora (for I later found out that was her name) arrived in the garden sometime between the doodlebug and the Korean War, decided she rather liked it and just stayed, morphing into a sort of tenant-heirloom, passed down from owner to owner. Not that I didn't find her absolutely enchanting, she was everything you could wish for if you were wishing for a nun. But I wanted to be on the safe side, so made sure she wasn't part of the deal before I tendered my offer.

But no, it transpired that she was in fact the current

CALL THE GREEN BERETS!

In the war against nature the Geneva Convention goes out the window. After battling with the forces of evil (remember the big scratchy jaggy things at the back door) for the best part of a decade, I decided to call in the troops. Also, I was never truly convinced Sister Eleanora had actually vacated the premises. I feared that one day I would discover her in the undergrowth, leading a tribe of Pygmy Nuns living off some whole new eco-system. Reinforcements would, I decided, be a good idea.

The troops came one by one under the guise of 'Garden Designer' – or some called themselves 'Consultant'. Each would arrive at their allotted time, gingerly walk through the garden on the only 'path' available – a pad made with my weekly trek out to the wheelie bin – and come back shaking his or her head. I knew from the start it wasn't good news.

'Was it an old person who lived here before you?' was the usual first question.

'Yes', I would reply, doing that nodding, tutting thing while raising my eyes to heaven, omitting the fact that they had left over a decade ago.

'Have you thought of turfing the whole thing over?' was another frequently asked question from the designer(s). (You get to know the FAQs in advance.)

Again my answer was 'yes,' adding, 'but that was such a rubbish idea I decided to call in a designer'. I think the humour was lost on them because few laughed at this. None really.

The consensus of opinion was that design alone would be £1000 (but the drawings would be in *coloured* pencil, so apparently this was a snip!) and the actual work anything in excess of £20k! (Using the K word apparently makes prices seem less hideous.)

So I did what any self-respecting radio-presenter strapped for cash would do: I called my local college (Langside), enquired about the garden design diplomas and signed up. And thus the desire to reclaim the garden began a life-long love affair with the soil.

***

I somehow managed to combine being a born-(yet)-again student with my work at the BBC, attending college on a full-time basis Monday, Tuesday and Wednesday, which left Friday, Saturday and Sunday free to work 2pm till midnight on the news-desk. No-one ever wanted to work this ungodly weekend shift pattern, so as a freelancer I was almost guaranteed work every week. I can't remember what I did on Thursdays. I was supposed to study but I think I either slept or went to Asda for the Big Shop. Anyway, I digress...

And so it was that 10 months later I emerged from

Woodburn Campus, diploma in hand, like a latter-day Capability Brown. A butterfly escaping from the cocoon. A Pygmalion of horticultural genius ready to re-design the gardens of the world.

I think in reality our class ran out en masse from the last exam and took refuge in the Kingspark Hotel, where the drink was remarkably cheap. Nonetheless, my new career as a Garden Designer and Horticultural Consultant was about to springboard. All I had to do was wait for the phone to ring. In anticipation I bought a drawing board. A big, sturdy muckle thing it was, freestanding and 6-foot high. Its sturdiness comes in handy even now, 10 years down the line, as it is still in use…as a makeshift coat rail!

FROM STICKY FINGERS TO GREEN FINGERS

(or...Big Butts & The Potting Shed...
No Life for a Grown Up!)

Ok, so I didn't become the grand-designer I'd planned to be. In truth, I was left cold by the reality of sitting each day in front of graph paper, designing green spaces for clients on a budget, especially as the remit was invariably little more than 'somewhere the weans won't get mangled and a place to put the whirlie-gig'.

But my time as a horty student was not wasted. Far from it. As a writer (of sorts – we don't all have to be James Joyce!) I gained a few commissions for gardening articles and to my surprise earned a reputation for being fairly knowledgeable in my field. (Pun entirely intended.)

I didn't really care about having a 'career' in horticulture. As a gardener I was hooked. I was outside every available moment. Up to my knees in mud, I would plant, prune, tweak and weed. I loved it.

Then one day out of the blue I got a call from the producer of *The Beechgrove Potting Shed*, BBC Radio Scotland's flagship gardening programme. They were apparently making some changes and doing a poll to see what people thought of the programme. Little did I know this was my first stage in the interview process.

I was asked onto the programme the following week to chat about growing cut flowers...which, as it turned out, was the second stage in the interview process. It must have gone fairly well, for within a month I was driving up to Aberdeen every Sunday to present the programme; a 300-mile round trip. But oh my goodness it was so worth it. What joy!

Getting paid to sit with Scotland's foremost experts and talk about gardening did NOT seem like work. In fact I think *I* would have paid *them* to do it. But apparently that was against NUJ guidelines and would have caused an uproar!

One of the best parts about being involved in the *Potting Shed* was working with some of the best names in Scottish horticulture – Jim McColl, Carole Baxter and Donald McBean to name but a few.

For those of you unfamiliar with the programme it's a sort of Scottish *Gardeners' Question Time*. I think the reason it struck a chord with the listeners was the fact it was so particular to Scotland's climate and soil conditions, which are so very different to those in the south of England, for example.

The experts' knowledge and advice was outstanding, and they genuinely took time and interest in each and every caller. Occasionally a question would stump the panel, whether through lack of information or because they'd been thrown a curveball about a plant that was foreign to them. In such cases they would pore over the question afterwards, consulting colleagues, books, the internet…anywhere they could find a solution. And, if possible, they would make sure the correct answer was given at a later date. And it was just brilliant to be able to talk to listeners every week about gardening.

Most weeks the programme was broadcast live from the Aberdeen studio, but occasionally it was pre-recorded at an outside location. Sometimes it would be an event like Gardening Scotland, or we would be invited to a local horticultural society. Whichever, I just loved getting to chat to listeners face to face.

Some of the questions at these events were hilarious. I remember an elderly man from Ayrshire who prefaced his question by telling us how he was sick and tired of his wife's ugly big butt! It transpired he meant the water butt in the back garden and wanted to know how he could disguise it. Trying to keep a straight face with that one was a nightmare, but I have a sneaking suspicion he knew what he was saying and enjoyed watching me bite my lip, going redder and redder.

'Corpsing' on-air – literally being speechless through laughter – was a big problem! Some of the experts were 'worse' than others when it came to making their fellow panellists laugh, and I'm thankful it was radio and not television because the tears streamed down my face on several occasions.

During these outside broadcasts there are often more questions *after* the event than during, and one of my all-time favourites was from a lady in Clarkston. We'd just finished recording at the local horty society, and as usual a wee crowd had gathered with queries that we hadn't had time to get to, or that enquirers had just been too shy to put their hands up to ask in open forum.

Anyway, this lovely lady said, 'Theresa, can I ask you a question?'

'Of course,' I replied.

'What is it you do for a living?'

'Eh, this,' I said. 'This is my job!'

'Oh! That's nice, Dear,' she said, and strolled off into the night, shaking her head, her face a picture, and clearly thinking *That's no job for a grown up*!

CHICKEN COOPS FOR THE SOUL!

For the most part, as a family we lived in the city, and when I moved into the cottage if felt like a sprawling country pile. Perhaps Mum thought so too, because the first week I was there she told me to get some chickens. 'You really need chickens,' she insisted. And she kept up this opening gambit at least once a week for the next 20 years.

It had always been Mum's dream to have a garden in the country with chickens running about in the yard outside. 'A few chickens will do you no harm,' she'd mutter under her breath when I refused to pander to her whim. The thought of keeping hens filled me with dread. Dirty, smelly, squawking birds that would have your eye out as quick as look at you.

Then something happened that changed my life forever.

We lost Mum.

Our Darling Mum, our Rock, our Hero. That impulsive, impetuous lady – who would try anything twice as long as she didn't get caught – passed away. She was 3 weeks short of her 89th birthday. We all thought she would live forever, but she passed away very suddenly one late-January morning and left a huge gaping hole in all our lives.

Dad had died just two years before, and it seemed as if we were only getting our breath back. Against the joy and massive good fortune of having two parents alive at a ripe old age is set the gnawing ache in the pit of your stomach that comes from the knowledge that you'll lose them both within a relatively short period.

This isn't the place for me to exorcise my feelings at that time, but amid the madness and mayhem of my grief I focused on one thing to try to keep me sane. I needed to get some chickens! If I was sure of anything, it was that.

I was already animal daft. But my devotion was mainly confined to cats. Apparently they're easy to look after. Whoever said that never had a diabetic cat that needed daily injections. I'll talk more about Chelsea another time!

Anyway, back to the chickens. It had been a long winter that had seen Scotland in the grip of a big freeze for 3 months. This enforced confinement gave me time to research every avenue of my new obsession, and stopped me thinking about what was really happening. I must have read loads of information on chicken husbandry on the World Wide Web, so as the snow cleared I was equipped with all the necessary knowledge for getting to grips with the chicken-keeping malarkey.

I concluded that for me the best thing would be to rescue ex-battery hens. This book isn't a platform for me to bang on about animals rights, or to try to emotionally blackmail you, Dear Reader...BUT if you could see the state of those poor wee mites, kept indoors, forced to lay every day of their short lives then slaughtered when a year old…well, you'd join my campaign quicker than I could say 'Linda McCartney'.

And it's actually quite fun rescuing chickens. It's full of intrigue and espionage. Let me tell you what happens.

As we know, battery hens are put into an environment where they're denied daylight and instead have artificial lights on 18 hours a day. That tricks them into thinking it's always is the laying season, thus forcing them to lay an egg every day. Once they're a year old they're pretty much done-in with all this (and who wouldn't be) and not as productive as they used to be, ergo, it's more profitable for the factory owner (I'm not calling him or her a farmer – I'm just not and you can't make me!) to send them off to be slaughtered, replacing them with new POL (point of lay) hens that will start producing eggs immediately.

We're talking about hundreds if not thousands of birds per operation. It's slicker to buy in all the birds at the same age – and thus dispose of them all at the same time too.

And this is where the British Hen Welfare Trust and other such charities come in. The main co-ordinator for each region negotiates 'rescuing' the hens from the factory person. Usually the co-ordinator needs a squad of volunteers to beg, borrow or steal some transport and take two or three hundred birds to a nearby barn, which is usually donated for the afternoon by a volunteer. With military precision you book in advance how many hens you're prepared to rescue, and turn up at the allocated barn at your allocated time. And that's that. It's all very last-minute and no-one knows until just a few days beforehand exactly where or when the great hen 'rescue' will take place. Once it's underway it's all done in the space of a few hours. If the volunteers can't grab the hens and transport them at the agreed time, then it's off to the slaughter house they go. Likewise if there is no available barn space – the operation can't go ahead and the birds are killed. It really is as cut-and-dried as that.

As luck had it (or not – to be honest this detail has no bearing on the actual outcome of the story), the BHW Trust co-coordinator for the area was my former news editor at BBC Radio Scotland. For me that made it all the more exciting somehow.

At home we prepared for weeks beforehand for the coming of the birds. I fenced off a section running the entire width of the back garden, giving me a chicken-run of 4 x15 metres. Then I pored over every design of chicken coop known to man. It was vital the girls had a bit of freedom: they'd spent their first year without ever seeing the light of day.

I was getting 6 birds, and couldn't see anything big enough to let them spread their wings. It was also important that it was easy enough to clean – I didn't want to have to fold myself in half or lie prostrate in a sea of mud – or chicken droppings – to do so.

In the end I plumped for a wooden children's playhouse, like a big Wendy house. It measured 6x6 feet (so, 36 square feet) and was also 6 feet tall (making it… eh…quite a lot of cubic feet it total), so I could stand up in it quite comfortably – even in high heels. (I'm a titch!)

The reason I'm being so exact with the size is that I could legally have kept 36 birds in that house! Yes, 36. Each bird would have had just 12 inches squared of floor space. And as long as I had provided food and clean water I would not have been breaking any law. This makes me think every time I read a food label that says 'adheres to animal welfare guidelines'.

So, the fence was up, the playhouse erected and wood shavings scattered on the floor. All I needed now were the birds.

The day of collection soon arrived and I was given the address of a barn close to the middle of Linlithgow, but not quite in it. It was somewhere else – no-one could quite remember the postcode.

I'm not sure what I expected when I arrived, but certainly not what I saw.

We trundled up the single-track road and the barn came into sight. It was huge. The door was open. And inside was the sorriest sight I had witnessed in a long time. Around 200 chickens, most with little or no feathers, were crammed inside. Some had what looked like bloodied beak marks on their bodies, others had lost an eye. Several dragged their feet as they walked. The state of these almost-bald birds was heart-breaking. Apparently they either pull out their own feathers through stress, or attack other birds and rip out their feathers. Their stress manifests itself as aggression.

All of those birds had been incarcerated for their entire lives, yet not one tried to escape through the open door. 'They don't know what outside is,' said Jim the BHW Co-coordinator.

Jim was from a farming family and still ran his own farm, so this was nothing new to him. For my part, I had been told what to expect. But that in no way prepared me for what I saw that day.

But before I could let sentiment get the better of me and attempt to take them *all* home, Jim packed 6 birds into the various cat baskets I'd brought with me, ready for the long drive. Luckily, all 6 of my girls had a full complement of eyes and working limbs. And I don't say that facetiously; I had no experience of looking after hens and I'm not a vet, so it was fortuitous for both parties that I didn't take on more than I could chew.

I stuck the baskets carrying my precious cargo in the back of my Citroën Berlingo – aptly, the sort of small van French farmers tend to drive, except that mine had windows. It was a scorching day and with the windows open off we went back to Glasgow. Jim waved us goodbye with the reassuring words, 'Don't panic, T.T., if they don't all survive the journey. Those birds have had a lot of stress.'

Bloody hell! That was the last thing I needed to hear. By this time *I too* was suffering from a hefty dose of stress, and wasn't sure *I'd* make the journey home.

It was such a weird sight. Those baldy birds really did look as though they ought to have been hanging in a butcher's window. They had no more than a dozen feathers between them.

I have to admit I did get a bit of a sinking feeling on the drive home. Had I taken on too much? But it was just for a fleeting moment. Looking at their wee faces, and knowing the hardship they'd suffered, my heart just melted.

I'm glad to say we all survived the journey. Back in Glasgow I put the girls safely in their new wee house and left the door wide open: it was such a glorious day and I couldn't wait for them to run around outside and enjoy their freedom.

Two hours later…I was still waiting for them to make an appearance. They refused to even stick a beak outside and huddled together in the corner, ironically taking up even less of the 12 inches squared of floor space for which the EU had legislated. I coaxed them with food, water…even promises of eternal happiness. But they wouldn't budge.

So I left them alone. And shortly afterwards, one lone chicken braved the outside world. She was like an alien creature, with no feathers and a long protruding neck.

(Oh and I have to tell you that picking up a live chicken with no feathers for the first time was the strangest thing ever. They feel unnaturally warm, and stubbly and soft and sharp all at the same time.)

Once the first hen ventured outside, the others soon followed. Only one refused to budge – she stayed indoors and stood on one leg, her head tucked under her wing. According to all the advice, she probably wouldn't last the night.

But I'm happy to say she defied the experts and within 24 hours was strutting her stuff outside with the rest of them.

I can't tell you how happy I felt watching them explore their new found freedom. Scratching the ground, running around, pecking the corn and meal from their wee buckets.

The one thing I hadn't realised about ex-battery hens was how friendly they are! I thought the lack of human contact would make them nervous and suspicious. But the opposite is true. Apparently they're bred to be docile and the poor wee things have no real understanding of danger. So within 2 days they were eating their food out of my hand.

The biggest joy of all was the way they rushed up to meet me as soon as I approached their pen. After a few days, I thought *Oh stuff it, I'll just let them have the run of the garden* and opened their pen to let them do their worst. It would be nice to say they understood the parts of the garden most precious to me and steered clear of my peony roses and hostas. It would be a joy to say they gobbled up the slugs and snails and other pests on my plot. But alas, Dear Reader, I was 'blessed' with the dumbest birds on the planet. The only chickens in the world that hated slugs. The precious worms on the other hand…those they would devour with gusto.

Within a week they'd broken into the kitchen and were terrorising the cats and stealing their food! My long-suffering 'other half', who had a long-standing fear of 'things with wings', would run off and bolt the door behind him, taking refuge with the cats.

Those chickens brought me more happiness than I ever thought possible. They made me smile out loud each and every day. Once they discovered the great outdoors they made the most of their freedom. Even when the rain came down in stair rods and bounced off the ground, they'd run around getting soaked, loving every minute of it. It must have been a novelty for them.

If I'm honest, those gorgeous girls were a godsend to me. I know on the face if it *I* rescued *them*, but in all honesty *they* rescued *me*. Mum was right – I did need some chickens in my life.

KILLER CHICKS AND THE SUBURBAN STAND-OFF

Until I kept chickens I didn't fully understand the phrase 'the passion of the converted'. But once my gorgeous girls were safely ensconced in my world there was no turning back. I loved everything about them and was hooked. I became the ultimate chicken-bore!

Every piece of literature I read was hen-related. Friends started buying me 'chicken-themed' gifts. The only thing I didn't do was get broody!

Not only were my girls soon eating out of my hand and coming running when I called them, I'm delighted to report that a few very short weeks later their feathers started to grow back. They filled out and their combs went from flaccid, pasty pink to a proud, luscious, vibrant red. I'm not sure how you can tell if a chicken is happy or not – they don't tend to smile and many would claim the brain of a chicken doesn't have sufficient sophistication or complexity to feel emotions – but I can assure you, those wee hens thrived on all that love and care and affection.

The cats, of course, were terrified. Unlike chickens, it's very easy to tell if a cat is happy or not! They eyed these newcomers with a mixture of disdain and fear. For them this was the ultimate revenge of the big-birds.

Initially I thought the hens would come under attack

from every cat in the neighbourhood, but not on your life! They squared up to just about any moggie that dared to cross their path.

Now, I love cats, but there was one particular neighbourhood feline that even I struggled to feel affection for. The only way to describe it was as a hissing ball of ginger fur. Any attempt to make friends with this fiend resulted in him launching himself at your face, fur standing on end and claws bared. In fact – and I swear this is no lie – he actually barred a young couple from getting into their own house one night. He stood in their porch and 'dared' them to take him on. This Suburban Stand-Off (a bit like a Mexican stand-off but more dangerous) went on for 20 minutes, with the hapless couple clinging together in the freezing cold until the owner was tracked down. This Mad Max of the cat world would surely try to kill or at least maim my gorgeous girls. You would think so, wouldn't you? Not a chance.

The one time the poor misguided creature pounced on what looked like easy meat – a lone hen that had strayed from the pack – he quickly realised he'd met his match. Quick as a flash, she turned and dug her claws in deep and viciously pecked his head while the other 5 ran to her aid and pitched in.

I was quite proud of their tough demeanour. Their 'don't mess' attitude. It sort of brought out the bad girl in me. They were fearless. I toyed with the idea of making them special sparkly jackets to wear, with 'Killer Chicks' embroidered on the back. A girl can dream can't she!

Nothing was too fierce for them. They saw off cats, squirrels and even a poor wee field mouse. That last one was actually my fault. I was turning my compost bin when a mouse scurried up through the pile and gave me a fright. I screamed like a big Jessie and, I kid you not, sensing I was in danger, one of the hens sprinted up from the bottom of the garden. I had no idea she could run as fast. And, before I could stop her, she pounced on the mouse, killed it with one mighty peck and swallowed it whole! I was stunned into silence. Gobsmacked. Despite my horror – revulsion actually – I was bursting with pride. Her loyalty and devotion was unquestionable.

Every time I tell that story – which is probably more often than is healthy – there's always some smarty-pants desperate to tell me that the hen was just a vicious killer and instinct caused her to attack the mouse. But if that was the case, why did she respond to my scream? And how did she even know the mouse was there? She was at least 40 feet from me and 2 terrace levels away. Nope, that wee hen sensed Mother Hen was in danger and stepped in.

I'll need to stop now. I fear I'm treading on very dangerous ground here!

On the whole I have to say the chickens were very easy to look after. But they do seem to like a lot of attention and human contact, so I wouldn't recommend it unless you're prepared to spend time with them.

And apparently they are not recommended if you live

in the Outer Hebrides. Lewis to be exact. It's the wind you see, plays havoc with them. Alasdair Fraser of BBC Alba is from that very part of the world and has a sorry tale to tell regarding his hens. By all accounts, during a particularly windy day they just blew away. The whole lot of them. And their hen-house. Poor Alasdair came home from school and all that was left was a big space in the garden and an even bigger space in his wee heart. There was never any sighting of the by now skyward hens, and they were never to be seen again.

Now, I know what you're thinking; the hens went off to that great hen-house in the sky via the Aga, and Mrs Fraser got shot of the hen-house on eBay. But Alasdair will hear none of it and to this day is convinced the birds just blew away!

***

Back to looking after the birds... (Who knows, one day you might need this information!)

They need to be let out at first light each morning, and no matter how smart your hens are they have no way of knowing that it's the 1st of January and that you'd rather lie in bed nursing a hangover than greet the day with a pile of chicken pooh. They also need to be safely and securely locked in each night. Once again they don't care if you have a night out organised, or want to go away for the weekend, or have a 4am start to your BBC travel shift. If you can't do it, you need to make sure you have someone else who can.

Then there's red mite, sour crop and wing clipping to be taken into consideration.

Luckily I had help. I met Stevie Harrison on a chance visit to Beeches Cottage nursery (near Lesmahagow), which he runs with his wife Margaret. I think it's fair to say horticulture is in their blood. Not only does Beeches have the most fantastic range of plants, it also has ducks and geese and sheep and goats and, above all else, chickens! The livestock, I have to add, is not for sale!

The Harrisons are probably what we now know to be 'people persons'! Their love of what they do comes first – their nursery is their passion. Stevie spends hours with customers, talking about plants and giving all sorts of sage advice (other herbs are available), and Margaret creates the most impressive hanging baskets I've ever seen. And each person who visits Beeches gets the same treatment, whether they buy one plant or a hundred.

Stevie was an absolute godsend to me. He gave me all sorts of top tips and handy hints and even drove through to Glasgow to fix a perch in my self-designed chicken coop (I hadn't realised that hens were roosting birds and needed to 'perch' at night). He also taught me how to deal with sour crop (I'll explain about that in a moment) and even clipped their wings.

The latter made me feel a bit queasy at first. I imagined it was painful, cruel and unnecessary to clip a chicken's wings – especially the wings of my gorgeous girls to whom I had promised a life of unbridled freedom. However you can have too much of a good thing, including freedom. Chickens don't make great flyers, but the wee rascals had picked up enough momentum to fly over the fence into next door's garden. No real harm done, I thought, but Stevie explained that there was a real danger one of them could get caught on the fence and seriously injured...or lost, or eaten by next door's dog, or captured by Colonel Sanders. Suffice to say he'd made his case and turned up with the sharpest pair of wing-clippers I've ever seen.

It was a quick and painless operation, I was assured. Hold the hen securely by the body, stretch out one wing and clip the feathers just past the point of growth. No worse than you or I getting a hair-cut – despite my horror stories of hair-cuts gone bad!

Stevie did 5 of the girls and they seemed none the worse for their ordeal. The shorter wings on one side meant they could still run around and flutter up to their perch but their flight path was reduced somewhat.

I was in charge of the last chicken. Stevie insisted that if I was to be this great hen-whisperer, then I needed to roll my sleeves up and get dirty.

I positioned the bird just like he said and fanned out her wing feathers in my hand. 'Now tell me the truth,' I asked, 'will this be at all painful?'

'Agonising,' Stevie replied, 'you've got your fingers trapped inside the blades!'

***

I'll end on a sour note, if I may. Or rather, a sour crop note.

Chickens store food in their 'crop' – a pouch at the base of their neck. In some cases, if the food is not digested it can ferment and become infected and the hen soon becomes poorly. It's fairly easy to detect – squeezing the crop will quickly tell you if it's full or not. If it is, you need to (carefully and don't do this if you don't have your own Stevie on hand to show you the ropes) hold the hen upside down and gently massage its throat until it vomits. If you hold the bird at the wrong angle, or let it vomit for too long, there's a danger it will choke.

Okay, so that's not the most glamorous thing you'll ever do, and to be honest you shouldn't have to do it very often, but it's a good gauge to see if chicken husbandry is for you!

IF MUSIC BE THE FOOD OF LOVE...

I'm truly blessed to be in a job that I love. I get to combine my passion for music, gardening and maps, mix them altogether, talk out loud on the wireless and call it work. Of course, I'm not saying I always love getting up at 4am, or working through the night, as have done on many occasions. (In fact I still feel slightly melancholy at the memory of the new Millennium, when I toasted the bells on my own during the overnight shift in Radio Clyde's newsroom.

But even that has it rewards. I rejoice reciting the tale, wearing my best martyred expression – handed down the female line of my family for generations – and gaining oodles of sympathy from anyone who cares to listen. (If only more would!))

Music has been part of my life for as long as I can remember. There was always music blaring in the background of our house, often from several sources. My dad could pick out a tune on just about any instrument, or so it seemed, but it was my mum and Julie Andrews who perhaps had the biggest influence on me – or, more accurately, my mum's obsession with Julie Andrews.

When I was four (a lot seemed to happen to me at this age!) *The Sound of Music* was in its heyday. Our family went along en masse, and although it wasn't really a kids' film, I rather liked some of the songs, the juggling with oranges and the silver screen interpretation of what life would be like if you had a nun to babysit during the summer holidays. It all seemed rather jolly.

The success of the film, and perhaps the dire lack of new releases during this period, meant the ABC in Sauchiehall Street screened a matinee performance of The Von Trapp Children every Tuesday afternoon. And I mean *every* Tuesday. The reason I know is that Mum decided this would be the perfect weekly jaunt for yours truly.

My siblings would be tucked in school, being taught by real nuns who bore no resemblance whatsoever to Julie Andrews and who, by all accounts, took no shit. This left my own Mother-Superior free to indulge her *Sound of Music* obsession.

Mum was charging headlong into becoming a lapsed catholic and this was her compensation for not going to mass. She dragged me along too, alas, convincing me it was a great treat.

And it was. Initially.

Getting to go to the pictures with just my mum was fabulous. After the first month I questioned if this film was mandatory viewing for 4-year-olds (okay, I may not have used the actual word 'mandatory' when aged 4), but she bribed me with chocolate, so I didn't complain. By the second month I was feigning illness and asking when I would be old enough to go to school. She said 'soon' and bribed me with even more chocolate – double rations now.

By the sixth month I had 3 fillings and was probably the only kid in Glasgow who dropped 'fjord every stream' into everyday casual conversation. By the end of the year it was time for me to go to school and the ABC Cinema replaced the matinee programme with something else. I don't know what, because Mum refused to discuss it and would 'fill up' every time I broached the subject.

Even today I can recite each and every word of dialogue and song lyric from that movie unprompted. I'm not sure it's a transferable skill though, so I don't tend to list it on my CV, but perhaps one day it'll come in handy.

I'm not saying those formative years had a bearing on my future career...but maybe they did.

***

Oh I've just thought of something. I'm going a bit off-piste here, I realise, but I need to tell you before I forget…

There are few memories more evocative than smell. A scent or an aroma can whisk you off to foreign climes in an instant, or transport you back to a long-forgotten childhood summer's day. For me, my favourite and most memorable smell was my baby's bottle. My Bok-Bok. My grandfather was in charge of mixing my formula and no-one could do it like he did. I enjoyed it so much I was almost 5 before I was finally weaned off this apparently manky habit. But the smell has always stayed with me. I miss that wonderful, sweet, comforting fragrance more than anything.

When children started appearing in our family – first from my sister, then my two brothers duly obliged – I couldn't wait for that smell to fill the house once more. But alas, the passage of time – or maybe it was a different formula – corrupted the aroma and it was nothing like I remembered. No matter how hard I tried, it just never smelled the same as when I was young.

Then one day, driving in the east end of Glasgow, that smell suddenly hit me. I couldn't believe it. I'd yearned for it for years.

'Oh smell that,' I cried to Mum and Dad, who were in the back seat. 'Babies' bottles!'

There was a stunned silence as they stared at each other, before declaring, 'Theresa, that's the whisky bond!'

LULU – SOMETHING TO SHOUT ABOUT!

I was a radio journalist in various newsrooms for over 10 years before I even considered producing music programmes. It was my (then) other half who pushed – or rather dragged – me into it. As a DJ and presenter, Paul had a particular genius for programme ideas. It must be said he also had an obsession with music, and that his obsession bordered on illness (his words not mine!). Anyway, he gained several commissions in a relatively short time to make programmes for BBC Radio 2, working in tandem with another production company. Discovering that he was particularly good at it, the natural progression was to branch out on his own. But he needed a PA and an editor.

During this time the BBC rolled out a new digital editing suite, which was in theory designed to unify the whole system across the network. They needed several trainers to 'teach out' this new technique and make sure everyone was up to speed given the opening of the new building at Pacific Quay in Govan.

And it's here my career took a wee meandering path, for I was seconded as a trainer.

When I was asked if I'd be interested in the post I jumped at the chance. As a freelancer I knew how important it was to widen my skill base *and* secure future work. The trainers were mainly BBC 'on-air' journalists, but as a rule journalists *don't* like to be taken off their patch for any period of time. I, on the other hand, liked the idea of being fairly itinerant and had no qualms about changing my role. It was something I was well used to.

It turned out to be a fortuitous move.

Prior to that, my editing skills were limited to compiling short news packs with sound effects. Or topping and tailing voice pieces and interviews to be used within a news bulletin. Like most journalists, I was self-taught in editing techniques, learning in the pre-digital age when we used tape, a stainless steel editing block and a razor blade.

There are few things more rewarding than splicing and editing tape, and many happy hours were spent in a dubbing room with what seemed like miles and miles of tape coiling round my ankles – and just as much, cut to size, hanging round my neck. I could lose myself for hours in an editing suite, until some big hairy editor screamed that he needed a piece of audio for the programme and I'd tear out with the finished article in hand – careful not to have put any reams of tape in upside down so it wouldn't come out like some dark satanic verse on-air.

No such fears with digital editing; it's all done with the click of a mouse, and any mistakes can be un-clicked just as quickly. But there's still a skill in editing – knowing just where that vital cut should go.

Initially I could only just keep one step ahead of those I was teaching. However, within a few months as a trainer, I was getting up to speed as a craft editor, and it seemed a natural progression to join forces with Paul on his new venture. Also, I was (just as in my Q96 days) cheap and available – a winning combination in any business partner. (Indeed, in *any* kind of partner!)

We started Five Cats Productions in the summer of 2008 – we had five cats at the time, hence the name. And within weeks we received our first commission from BBC Radio Scotland, *Lulu: Still Shouting at 60!* It was to be a celebration of the singer's life in her landmark year.

We still argue over whose idea it was. Paul said of course it was his as he was the brains of the operation! But in truth, Dear Reader, it was my idea and I'm writing it here in black and white as proof for all to see. (The views of this book are strictly my own and may not adhere to either fact or the opinions of others!)

The memory of making our first programme together still gives me a warm fuzzy glow inside. The wonderful Kaye Adams conducted the interview and thus fronted the programme.

Lulu was the consummate professional; she arrived on time, answered each question candidly and came across as a very astute businesswoman who has worked hard for each and every ounce of her considerable success.

The programme charted her 45-year career in the industry and uncovered a few surprises. She revealed that she hated *Boom Bang-A-Bang* (her Eurovision joint-winner of 1969 – 4 countries shared top spot that year) and *I'm A Tiger*, and said her mum was 'fizzin mad' when she first went down to London and developed an English accent!

I know Lulu gets a lot of stick for her accent, but in her defence it should be remembered that she went down to London as a teenager in the 60s, when there were few, if any, regional accents on TV; and, unlike today, back then Glasgow accents were just not considered 'cool'. She lived with her manager Marion Massey, who was posher than the Queen Mother, and suddenly this wee lassie from Dennistoun was meeting the likes of Frank Sinatra and trying to 'fit in' with The Beatles. Is it any wonder she clipped and modified her voice?

Lulu: Still Shouting at 60 was the flagship programme for BBC Radio Scotland's festive season and was broadcast on New Year's Day 2009. We were chuffed to bits.

SAVING THE LAST DANCE...
FOR ANDY WILLIAMS

Our next programme together was my favourite ever project up to that point, and I think it still is to this day. *Can't Get Used to Losing You: The Untold Story of Pomus & Shuman* celebrated the lives and careers of the song-writing duo Doc Pomus and Mort Shuman. They had over a thousand songs to their name and wrote hits for Andy Williams, Elvis Presley and Ray Charles to name but a few.

One of their most famous numbers, *Save The Last Dance for Me*, was of course a huge hit for The Drifters. We were fortunate that both Doc & Mort's families agreed to contribute to the programme, and we're still in contact with Doc's daughter, Sharyn Felder. It gave us a special insight into the writing of many of the songs, and I'm still moved to tears when I recall the story behind the lyrics to this particular one.

Born in 1925 in Brooklyn New York, Doc Pomus was 11 years older than his song-writing partner Mort Shuman. He'd contracted polio as a child and, as a result, walked with braces and a crutch, eventually ending up in a wheelchair.

In 1957 he married Broadway actress Willie Burke. Since Doc was Jewish and Willie catholic, the wedding was a quiet family affair with a small reception afterwards.

Unable to dance because of his disability, Doc watched as Willie danced with his brother, his father, cousin and even Mort. And as he sat at the table and watched his new bride on the dance floor, he idly penned the lyrics to this now famous song. '...*don't forget who's taking you home...and in whose arms you're gonna be...Darling, save the last dance for me.*'

We interviewed Willie for the programme and she was in tears as she recalled how years later she found the menu from that day among Doc's belongings, with the words scribbled in pencil in his handwriting.

The wonderfully talented Shuman scored the music for this hit, which initially appears to be a catchy up-beat number with a slight bossa beat; until you understand the sentiment behind the words and realise it's one of the most heartfelt and poignant modern love songs of the 20th century.

Everyone we spoke to agreed that Doc Pomus was a wonderful man with a huge personality. He was friends with and influenced so many people in the music industry, including Bob Dylan, Ben E King and Phil Spector. In fact his daughter recently told me that his home town of Brooklyn is naming a street Pomus Place in his honour.

***

It was this story that captivated the imagination of the commissioning editors when we first approached BBC

Radio 2 with the programme idea. They agreed it would make a great documentary – as long as we got a big name to present.

'How about Andy Williams,' I suggested. Andy had of course had his biggest hit of 1963 with *Can't Get Used to Losing You*, another Pomus & Shuman classic.

Meanwhile my stomach was going like a washing machine and we both had our fingers crossed underneath the table, not believing we'd ever get him in a million years!

The men in suits agreed to commission us, but with one important caveat: no Williams, no programme!

'It's in the bag,' I lied, my knees shaking as we left, wondering how the hell we were going to get such an American legend to work for two novice documentary-makers from Glasgow.

I have to admit when I blurted out his name as a possible presenter I wasn't even sure if he was still alive!

One of the good things about being a journalist is that I can find contact details for almost anyone on the planet. It transpired that not only did Andy Williams own the Moon River Theatre in Missouri, but he still performed at the restaurant there almost every day, despite being 82 at the time.

So it was with some trepidation that I called the Theatre and asked if I could speak to his agent. His PA, Julie, was just lovely and we chatted for a few minutes before she said, 'Why don't I just connect you straight through to Mr

Williams!'

My legs nearly went from under me. I was a nervous wreck waiting to be put through. I couldn't believe I was actually going to speak to him direct. Then suddenly he was on the line, 'Hello, this is Andy Williams.'

I would have recognised that voice anywhere. Older, of course, but still that same familiar drawl from when he was a regular on the telly-box during my childhood.

I'm afraid in an attempt to sound very cool, calm and collected my nerves got the better of me. I speak quickly at the best of times, but on this occasion my voice was a freight train. I was hell-bent on saying my piece. I had a sort of pre-rehearsed script and went into overdrive trying to convince him why he just *had* to get on board with this project.

I spoke for a solid ten minutes – a long time if you're on the receiving end – barely taking a breath. But why stop there? I was on a roll and just kept going. He didn't interrupt, so was clearly very impressed by my spiel. (Or so I like to think). No matter how much I tried to control my tempo I was ninety miles an hour. Never mind, it meant I could cram more into the 'conversation'.

I eventually drew to a close after fifteen minutes, happy that I had done a more than decent pitch and he'd be insane to turn us down. I took a deep breath and let Mr Williams speak. And I'll never forget those momentous words... 'I'm sorry,' he said. 'Do you speak English?'!

Miraculously, after employing the help of an interpreter

he agreed to take part. We agreed a recording date for Mr Williams (I *never* called him Andy when speaking to him, I was way too shy), secured interviews with the families of both Pomus & Shuman and even had a transmission date. We were good to go.

We must have recorded over one hundred hours of interviews (all for two 57-minute programmes), spent weeks trawling through archive audio and were lucky enough to have Sharyn Felder send us over rare never-before-broadcast interviews her dad did throughout his life.

The hardest part of the whole project was deciding what to leave out. We could have made a 6-part series with the material we had. And, while listening to the thousands of songs they wrote, I realised that Pomus & Shuman not only changed the musical landscape at the time, but provided the soundtrack for the lives of a whole generation of teenagers.

But theirs was not just a catalogue of throw-away pop songs. Doc wrote of his own experiences in many of his songs, though for those who did not know his backstory that might not have been immediately obvious. Let me give you a couple of examples.

Teenager In Love – one of their first hits – was originally entitled *It's Great to be Young and In Love*. We had access to the original recording of Doc & Mort actually singing the demo of this up-beat number in their office at The Brill Building. It sounded nothing like the finished article. Doc was by then on the wrong side of 30 but remembered his teenage years with sorrow and angst. For him it had been anything but great to be young and in love. He'd walked with the aid of crutches, had been overweight and in poor health and had not felt confident around girls his age. And with this insight they crafted the heartfelt ballad of *Teenager In Love*, capturing perfectly the anxiety and torture he had experienced at that age. Clearly it hit a chord with the fans and was a huge hit.

We also discovered from Doc's ex-wife Willie that not only was she the muse for *Save The Last Dance For Me* but Doc penned the lyrics of *Can't Get Used to Losing You* when it was obvious the couple were heading their separate ways.

It's enough to make you cry!

When we got round to recording Andy Williams he revealed that despite *Can't Get Used To Losing You* giving him one of the biggest hits of his career he hated the song, and came close to not recording it! Initially he had refused to sing it, describing it as 'dirge-like' and saying no-one would buy it. It was his agent who convinced him just to give it a go, telling him to try it out during one of his performances before actually cutting the disc. It was only when he heard the arrangement with those haunting pizzicato strings that he relented and thought *maybe* it wasn't so bad. But even almost 50 years later, when I told him the song remained one of my all-time favourites, he expressed doubts... 'Do you *really* like it?' he asked, never truly convinced he'd made the right choice.

They say you should never meet your heroes as you'll only be let down. But I'm delighted to say that Andy Williams lived up to all my expectations and delivered his lines like a pro.

The recording completed, as producers we crafted the programme from the hours of audio we had – cherry-picking the best bits, laying them all down in the correct order to ensure the story flowed. Only then did we write Mr Williams' script, letting his narrative drive the story forward. The trick is to keep the voice-over short, allowing the music – and of course the contributors – to help it all unfold. I have to say that Andy was a joy to work with, and was happy to do as many re-takes as were necessary, though thankfully very few were required.

Logistically, it proved impossible to meet him in person and all the recording had to be done using 2 studios; Mr Williams was in Missouri while we were in…glamorous Govan! Some you win, some you lose!

After the recording we chatted and he said he was delighted to be involved in the programme. He was witty and charming and just lovely, and seemed genuinely chuffed that we were fans – we'd been to see him perform in Glasgow a few years prior.

By now, of course, I had learned to speak at half my normal speed, complete with a dodgy American twang, all to make sure he understood me. Which he did, because after the programme was finished he congratulated me on my English…and said I was showing signs of great improvement!

Andy Williams was diagnosed with cancer shortly after the programme was made and died less than 2 years later. It was a real honour to work with such a legend and I treasure the photograph he sent us on which he wrote:

Hey Paul & Theresa,

It was real fun working with you guys.

Andy

WHEN THE RHINESTONE COWBOY CAME TO GOVAN

My only regret about making the *Can't Get Used To Losing You* programme was during an interview with Glen Campbell.

The Rhinestone Cowboy was performing in Glasgow and had dropped into BBC Scotland for a Radio 2 interview. I caught sight of him as he sauntered across the corridor of Pacific Quay. He was 75 years old but still looked incredibly cool. And I swear he was at least 7 feet tall. Well maybe not *that* tall, but he was huge, with the biggest shoulders I've ever seen.

It suddenly struck me that when he sang with The Beach Boys they covered *Hushabye*, a Pomus & Shuman song originally written for The Mystics. It was a very tenuous link but I realised it might sound good in the programme.

He had just completed his Radio 2 slot and was on his way out the door when, ever the opportunist, I grabbed him and talked him into speaking to me for a few minutes. I don't think he realised he could have said no! He seemed to think this was all pre-arranged. The only trouble was I was supposed to be on a travel shift…

I say 'supposed to be'… In fact, I was *actually* on a travel shift. So not only did I persuade/force Glen into this impromptu interview, I actually made the poor man wait and listen while I told the rest of Scotland how busy it was on the M8! Surprisingly, he seemed to rather like it.

Glen Campbell was absolutely delightful. Nothing was too much trouble for him, and his wife who was with him was just gorgeous. She too was really accommodating and assured him he had more than enough time to have a wee chat with me.

He was hilarious. When I asked if his family came on tour with him, he said some of the kids did. When I asked how many children he had, he shrugged his shoulders. 'Heck, I don't know.' Then, turning to his wife, he said, 'Hey Honey, how many kids do we have?'

'Eight', she replied.

He did one of the best double takes I have ever seen. 'Jesus, we've got eight kids? No way!'

Anyway, unfortunately he couldn't remember the song *Hushabye* and it transpired he had never actually recorded it, only sang it occasionally on tour. (I probably should have checked the facts before pinning him down, but I'd had to think on my feet.) But we had a nice chat about other things – mainly Elvis – and it turned out that he had been a session musician on *Viva Las Vegas*, another Pomus & Shuman track. Bingo! But try as I might I couldn't get him to actually talk about the songs, he just reminisced about all the wonderful things he and Elvis had got up to.

It was a great interview but none of it was suitable for the documentary. That's not the part I regret though. I can hardly bear to write down what I regret most.

We (Me 'n' Glen!) were sitting in the studio, with the engineer recording everything. He was plucking on his guitar and bursting into spontaneous song, which was just wonderful.

'Remind me again what song you're talking about?' When I reminded him it was *Hushabye* he asked me to sing it; he would play it.

Now let me tell you, when it comes to singing I am not shy. I'm not a brilliant singer, but I can sort of hold a tune and have been known on many an occasion to have a wee drink and sing *On Mother Kelly's Doorstep*. So I normally don't get embarrassed about singing in front of people. But jamming with Glen Campbell…that was too much! At that very moment I was gripped by an attack of nerves so severe I could only splutter out, 'I can't, I'm shy!'

He tried to cajole me into singing and each time I refused. My face was burning scarlet and I just couldn't bring myself to start.

Now, remember that an engineer was recording all this with some of the best sound systems available. And what did I do? I gave up the opportunity of a lifetime, that's what: the chance to sing along in an acoustic session with Glen Campbell. I'm still kicking myself. And have the bruises to prove it.

ENID, FANNY & THE BROTHERS GRIMM

I was going to say I've always loved reading, but that's not true. As a child I inherited my siblings' *Famous Five* books, which they seemed to devour in a frenzy but which left me cold I'm afraid. Enid Blyton did nothing for me.

My two brothers and sister were 'great readers' by all accounts, but I didn't seem to inherit the bookworm gene. I scanned the pages, taking hours over each chapter, but the meaningless words just swam about on the page. It was obvious I just couldn't read. Oh I could do the nuts and bolts of reading – individual words – but actually getting through even the shortest of children's books? For me it was like trying to nail jelly to a wall.

Then one day at a jumble sale (we made our own entertainment as 7-year-olds in those days!) I saw a dog-eared green leather bound book with 'curly writing' on the front. Shallow to the core, and always judging books by their covers, I bought it because it was only thr'pence and looked sort of interesting. And when I say that it looked 'interesting', I mean the physical appearance of the book, not the stories inside.

It turned out to be a collection of short stories by Hans Christian Andersen. Some of the titles I recognised – *The Little Mermaid*, *The Red Shoes*, *The Tin Soldier* – they were already part of my psyche and I had come across them individually, or in nursery tales. But here they were, about 40 stories in all, bound together in one single volume.

I was mesmerised as I flicked through the pages. This was bloody brilliant! Forget your *Famous Five* with Fanny, lashings of ginger beer and Timmy the Dog. Who needed that rubbish when I had passion, intrigue, jealousy, rage... you name it, it was there in that interesting green tome with curly writing.

After that I progressed to the Brothers Grimm. I was well and truly hooked, and realised that the fairy tales we were all told in our childhood were far from innocent nursery stories.

The 'Enid Blyton Bashing' began not long after that. (Others did the bashing, not sweet, innocent me. Honest!) Britain's most famous children's author of the 20th century was derided as a politically incorrect racist, bigoted snob. I felt a bit sorry for Enid's family if truth be told. However, I didn't feel sorry for Enid herself – the accusations came out posthumously, too late to affect her directly, and by which time she'd made enough dosh to keep her in lashings of ginger beer for all eternity.

Secretly I rather liked that her scribbling left me cold. Recently, at a book festival, I heard one woman say almost the very same thing. 'I could never relate to Enid Blyton stories,' she said. 'I'm from the west of Scotland, where Fanny means only one thing!"

Oh how I wish I'd said that!

THE MAGIC OF *THE MAGUS*

It's always hard to decide what your favourite book is. It's like your favourite song or your favourite film or your favourite plant…it really depends what mood you're in, so the choice can change daily or hourly.

Straight off the bat I usually say *Jane Ayre*…until I remember *Wuthering Heights*, then perhaps *Great Expectations*. But for me one gem always comes back into my top ten: *The Magus* by John Fowles.

I'd read *The Collector* by the same author after watching the film on telly as a kid. Probably not suitable viewing for a 12-year-old, but I had childhood insomnia and it was all that was on at the time. Then one summer I was going to Greece on holiday. I'd been backpacking there several times prior and fancied doing some more island-hopping. So nothing was really planned, and anyone who knows me can confirm that I travel light. I'd be a useless drugs mule – I normally only carry one tiny bag and have been known to throw away clothes en route if my pack becomes too heavy. Anyway, I popped round to a friend the night before the flight and she gave me a novel to read while I was away. 'It's set in Greece,' she said, 'so you might like it. And it's thick,' she added, 'so should last you the week.'

I took this great 600-page tome, which probably

weighed more than my entire luggage. (This was pre-Ryanair when you could actually get on a plane carrying a case that weighed two ounces more than a meringue.)

I started reading it on the flight and have to say that initially I didn't like the main protagonist – a spoiled brat called Nicholas Urfe – but since it was set in Greece, and since that was where I was heading, I kept going. And as the story unfolded I became more and more engrossed in the plot. Intrigue, mystery, magic even; right up my street!

The book was set on the fictional island of Phraxos, where Urfe taught English at a boys' school. It sounded idyllic.

All that had been agreed about the trip was that we'd get to Athens then decide which islands we'd visit from there, essentially following our noses. One of the islands we ended up on was Spetses. It was fairly unspoiled at the time and was an absolute joy. I settled down on one of its deserted beaches to continue reading *The Magus*. As John Fowles described the school – a grand building, with statues outside and huge wrought iron gates – I glanced up and could actually picture the scene. Indeed I could literally (in both senses of the word) picture it!

Because not 200 yards from the beach, across what counted as the main road for the island at the time, was a building that scarily resembled Fowles' narration. Everything about it was identical, even the small winding road that led to the bakers down at the bottom of the street. Bloody hell, I could even smell the bread! It really was just as he'd described it!

I asked about (making early use of my yet-to-be-discovered journalistic talents), and sure enough the building across the street had once been a very well-to-do boys' school. And further investigation revealed that the fictional island of Phraxos was indeed Spetses.

You see, unbeknownst to me, Fowles had been an English teacher on a Greek island and had based much of the book on his experience there. And I had found myself reading his booking directly opposite the very school in which he had taught, on the very same spot from which he must once have viewed it. No wonder it matched the description!

The school had closed (in 1983, I think) and had become a government building, but it was exactly as in the book. Every minute detail.

I walked along the winding road...and, sure enough, there at the bottom was the local baker's shop, where bread and pastries were being baked, as they had been for generations.

I'm not sure if this coincidence had any great cosmic meaning, but I always felt a special affinity with the book and story after that. I certainly didn't *plan* to read a book set in Greece and I had no way of knowing that the one my friend had given me was set on Spetses...and I certainly had no way of orchestrating that I'd be reading that particular chapter at the very time I was opposite the very scene it described. It just all seemed to fit so well – as though it was meant to be.

(Of course, my friend chose the book about Greece because that's where I was headed, so that wasn't a coincidence. But there must be hundreds – even thousands – of books set in Greece, even if you limit the choice to those in English... No, no, I'll stop rationalising. I'm spoiling the memory.)

Having said that I loved the book, parts of it flash back to the resistance during the Second World War, and I'm afraid those gave me the most terrible nightmares. Even today, the most benign novel set in wartime can spark off a series of bad dreams!

LAUGH? I THOUGHT I'D NEVER START!

'When I first said I wanted to write comedy everyone laughed... They're not laughing now!'

(Bob Monkhouse)

I would like to say it's a funny thing writing comedy. It *should* be. After all, you're writing words that (with a bit of luck) will make people laugh. But 'merry-making' is harder than many imagine. In truth, writing comedy can be a lonely job, with angst and stress the only companions. And it can bring out all sorts of neuroses and insecurities in even the sanest of people.

(Actually, that last bit isn't strictly true. The 'sanest of people' have absolutely *no* desire to write comedy and are very happy as they are thank you.)

Of course, like most of my adult pursuits, writing comedy certainly beat working for a living, but it was a slog nonetheless!

And my career as a comedy writer was rather short-lived, that's true. But at least it *did* live.

I hit a bit of a purple patch early on in my endeavours to make people merry...but, like so many things in my life, it was more through accident than design.

In my head I'd been a writer for as long as I could remember. For years I'd been scribbling away with very little success.

(I've just remembered that I actually had a weekly column in the Pa*isley Daily Express*. I had completely forgotten about that! Which is not a surprise given that my weekly words of wisdom were unceremoniously dropped like a hot stone, to be replaced firstly by an article about a woman with Paisley's biggest fridge-magnet collection and, from there on in, by the weekly round-up of Local Church news. No wonder I blocked the whole thing out like a bad dream. Oh the ignominy of it all!)

I suppose writing radio news bulletins and scripts every hour – on the hour – of my working day might suggest that I was actually 'writing'. But writing and 'being a writer' are two very different things.

What I really wanted to do was write 'proper stuff' – to hone my craft, write words that would make people sit up and take notice. What I wanted to write was comedy. And I like a good chuckle, so how hard could it be?

My love of comedy probably stems from my dad. And I'm sure my siblings will agree with this. Despite the fact he was shy and quiet and hated being the centre of attention, Dad – Stephen Talbot – was one of the funniest men on the planet. He had a wicked sense of humour; and when mixed with his quiet persona it was deadly.

Dad was also a very keen photographer and took

cine-films (this was pre-video days) of any and every family event. (And a 'family event' was often just us weans running around Kelvingrove Park, with Mum in the background either knitting (which I'm sure must have been staged, because Mum was a rubbish knitter), lighting a fire or preparing food. (The Talbots never went anywhere without a picnic!) And then, when the telly was rubbish (most nights!), he'd get out the projector and show old home movies as well as an array of comedy classics: Charlie Chaplin, Laurel and Hardy, Harold Lloyd. All without sound. In fact we must have had hundreds of hours of those old 8mm movies stored in the classic round, discus-like metal containers.

Those movie nights were great. We had a portable canvas screen that I remember as huge, but which was probably no more than 4 by 6 feet. Inevitably, at some point the film would 'stick' in the projector and melt, such was the heat from the bulb. Then it was panic stations. The film had to be retrieved from the projector before the celluloid actually caught fire; the damaged piece had to be cut out and the remaining part threaded back through the cogs to get the film on the screen again. Thinking of it now, it was all quite posh.

We certainly weren't posh, but we were lucky. (I know you're probably thinking a house full of weans with deadly flammable material was all a bit more 'deadly' than posh…and that our luck was in not having our house burn to the ground around us!) Those movie nights, with the silent-comedy greats in our living room, would have us all in stitches.

In fact, Dad said he actually 'met' Laurel and Hardy during their 1952 and 1953 stage tours of Britain and Ireland – though 'saw' would be more accurate. The stars would both have been in their 60s by that time, with their heyday a long-distant memory. But they still attracted a huge crowd at the Olympia Theatre in Dublin in May 1952. (Did I tell you my parents were from Dublin?) To many fans they were still heroes, even if heroes of a bygone age.

But I'm sad to report that Dad didn't give the comedy duo a glowing report, saying they had little time for their fans outside the theatre. He even alluded to them possibly having been drunk, and – worse still – to them using foul language! Our dad was a real gentleman and stickler for manners, and any misdemeanour or 'language' of that type would have horrified him.

SOMETHING FOR THE WEEKEND?
ARE YOU HAVING A LAUGH?

So it came to pass that in our house we all grew up on comedy, from the early Hal Roach and Mack Sennet stables (the key comedy producers of their day) to the 'modern-day' Morecombe and Wise, Tommy Cooper and Spike Milligan. *I'd love to make people laugh*, I thought as I watched. At the time I had no idea 'other people' – script writers – were often behind the scenes, crafting each word, each movement to make it all seem natural.

And gradually, as the years passed, I came to think, *I can do that. Writing comedy? What a spiffing wheeze.* Or so I thought...

I had no idea that every word, every phrase, every scene has not just to be written, but then re-written, 'passed' by a producer, sent back to the writer because it's 'just not funny', then re-written again...ad infinitum. Even proper big grown-up comedy writers have to go through this tiresome process. *Fawlty Towers* is comedy genius, but John Cleese is quoted as saying that each episode went through at least a dozen re-writes before they got it just right.

Back to the genesis of my short career as a comedy writer...

I was in the hairdresser's one day. (This is turning into one those Ronnie Corbett stories that go off at so many tangents that the original thread is lost among the mayhem.) Anyway…I was in the hairdressers one day and fortuitously enough sat beside a chap who was indeed himself a comedy writer. George (the hairdresser) introduced us, as was the polite thing to do at that time. (I have to say George the hairdresser ran a very eclectic salon and clients were often on first name terms with each other by the time the first tendril was teased.) The person George introduced me to was Ricky Brown, who was a columnist with *The Sun* and also part of the Comedy Unit, which provided much of BBC Radio Scotland's comedy programmes.

'I'd like to write comedy,' I said.

To his credit, Ricky didn't roll his eyes. But he didn't have much hair, so I knew I had to be quick or he'd soon be out the door and my opportunity would be lost forever. I had to cut to the chase.

'What do I do?' I asked.

I was actually overwhelmed by Ricky's generosity. He gave me the name of a chap at the Comedy Unit to whom I could send my stuff, and gave me his own email address, *and* even offered to cast an eye over anything first before I submitted it.

The Comedy Unit wrote and produced *Watson's Wind-Up*, a topical sketch show based on the week's events. It was filmed each Friday at the Glasgow Film Theatre, edited that afternoon, then broadcast the next day on BBC Radio Scotland. This seemed like the perfect place to start: I was a freelance broadcast journalist at the very same station, so knew all the topical news stories, and I wanted to write comedy. All I needed to do was listen through some back-episodes of *Watson's Wind-Up*, study the form, then trawl through the news of the past week to get some nuggets of humour. Easy peasy.

And it was. Or so it seemed. My first sketch was based on the 'five a day' adverts bouncing around that told people how much fruit and veg they should eat if they didn't want to collapse in a pool of their own congealed arteries. I emailed off the one-minute sketch (any longer than a minute and they need to pay you more) and waited…and waited.

I heard nothing. Almost two weeks passed and I thought I'd listen in again to *Watson's Wind-Up* to see which funny stories were making the news that week. Alas, I only caught the tail end of the programme…in which the writing credits were read out:

'…and this week's show was written by…blah blah blah…Theresa Talbot…and blah blah blah…'

Sweet Mother of God!!! I nearly passed out! I had actually had a joke broadcast on the radio!!! And not just *any* joke…my *first* joke. I was delighted.

A couple of days later I got an email from the Comedy

Unit to say my joke was actually 'performed live' a few days after I sent it in, but was edited out of the broadcast programme because of time constraints. However (and honest to God this is the truth) they thought it was so funny they decided to run it again the following week to ensure it went out on-air.

The joke was meant to be 'performed', so it may lose something in the written word and I can't find the actual transcript, but it went something like this...

PHONE RINGS

WOMAN *(40 a day voice – coughs and splutters)*: Hello?

MAN *(Bit anxious)*: Oh hello – I was hearing about this 5-a-day thing and I'm wondering how I can eat more fruit and veg.

WOMAN: No problem. See when you're eating yer chips, make sure you take plenty of tomato sauce.

MAN: Oh aye...

WOMAN: And then for yer pudding, instead of chocolate, why not have a wee strawberry tart?

MAN: Aye...great...

WOMAN: Then for a snack, a wee bar of Cadbury's Fruit 'n' Nut, then in the evening ditch that pint and take a wee tot of orange in yer vodka...

that's yer 5 a day totally sorted.

MAN: Oh man...thanks that's great...

WOMAN: No problem – speak to you later...and thanks for calling Healthy Living Scotland!

Jonathon Watson and his team made it sound hilarious, so I sent in another one. This time the joke was a wee bit smutty – about the Anglican Church allowing gay priests to be ordained. Again they used it and for a second time there I was among the proper big grown up writers with my name in the credits at the end of the programme.

TEARS, TANTRUMS
AND TUMBLEWEED!

With two jokes in two weeks and a one hundred percent hit ratio (we have to hang on to these small victories), I'm sure you can guess what I did next!

Yes that's right. I blanked. I couldn't think of another funny thing to say. Not one.

Once again I sat in front of a clear screen – white enough to give me snow blindness – until I convinced myself that even if I *did* get something onto paper, and even if I *did* pluck up the courage to send it off, it wouldn't be any good…and then the producers would think I thought I was funnier than I was…and then they'd feel really sorry for me, then they'd be mortified for me and… Just go back to the top of this section where I speak about comedy-writing bringing out insecurities and neurosis!!!

In the months and years that followed I did dabble a wee bit in comedy-writing. I kept my ear to the ground for any workshops I could attend, and lo and behold up popped a one-day workshop at the BBC (open to staff and civilians alike) for budding comedy-writers. That day put me on the radar of Margaret Anne Docherty, who was a comedy producer for Radio Scotland. She obviously saw something in my ideas and I was invited to submit to *The Why Front*, again a BBC Radio Scotland sketch show recorded in front a live audience. My comedy career was resuscitated!

Again, I had a fair wee bit of success, and became a regular writer on the programme. I even managed to write a 45-minute comedy – *Spooks and Sporrans* – a sort of 'horror news spoof' – which went out at Halloween. Sadly that sank without a trace, and I don't think I'm being harsh on myself to say the listening figures struggled to reach double digits. In my defence, Your Honour, it was on at the same time as a ginormously huge massive great big major cup final football match thing that was being broadcast on both telly and AM radio at the very same time. I ask you! Who could compete with such a thing? (And who could ask for a better excuse for low listenership!)

But all good things come to an end. *Watson's Wind-Up* and *The Why Front* popped their respective clogs, and, with them, my comedy-writing career also came to an end.

I was always too feart to try any other outlets. I don't think I was scared of failure – on the contrary, I sort of expected it! I think I was actually scared of success. What really terrified me was the thought of doing it well once, then being expected to repeat that success again and again. Apparently 'fear of success' is a very real and recognised phobia; great scholars and academics have written theories and theses on that very subject. You never know what kind of affliction you'll be landed with!

***

I'd like to add a wee post-script to this – and I'm not sure of its relevance to this book, but I'd like to say it anyway.

Despite Dad's wicked sense of humour and very dry wit, I can honestly say I never heard him swear or use any kind of bad language. He did use 'bloody' with alarming frequency – it seemed to trip off the tongue rather easily. But 'bloody' doesn't count as swearing, does it?

I'm sure the four of us must have been quite a handful at times – at one point Mum had 3 babies under the age of 3 in the house – yet despite this I never heard my dad raise his voice, let alone raise his hand to any of us. And likewise we were never cheeky to him nor gave him any kind of back-chat. It just wasn't an option. He was such a gentleman; it would have seemed just…well, wrong somehow to have been cheeky to Dad. He'd have been mortified. *We*'d have been mortified. My mother, on the other hand, was a holy terror. But let's not dwell on that.

And I do want to get serious for a moment and just say to any dads out there: be careful how you act around your children. Well, daughters actually. For you will very probably be the blueprint by which, in the future, they judge men. I make no apologies if that seems trivial or old-fashioned or sexist. It's a fact. And that's that. And I'm not just talking about finding a mate – her mate could be of any gender. Och, you know what I'm talking about: kindness begets kindness and all that malarkey.

Which brings me neatly on to Charity Begins At Home... I know we bend and shape this to suit when we're suffering from charity fatigue – which is now a very real ailment might I add. But in this great big world, with all the bad things that happen, we can all do our wee bit to make things that little bit nicer. An act of charity is basically an act of love. A home full of love and kindness will produce off-spring who are also full of love and kindness.

And while I'm feeling all warm and fuzzy, I need to mention a lovely story I heard the other day. My friend's mum – who is now in her 80s – was talking about her father back in Ireland. There wasn't much money to go around, but the house was always full of love, and he told her one thing that she remembers to this day: 'Never borrow or ask someone for money; but if you have any at all left over, give it to someone who needs it.' I just thought that was a lovely sentiment.

It goes without saying that we were heartbroken when Dad was reaching the end of his time. And in the days and weeks before he left us, we four siblings camped out in his hospital ward, taking turns holding his hand, telling stories, keeping a vigil. It's no surprise that we got to know the staff quite well.

One nurse remarked what a gentleman Dad was, and said that every member of staff thought so. And as we reminisced, I told her he was from Dublin, which came as a surprise to her.

'Couldn't you tell by his accent?' I asked.

But sadly by this time Dad was no longer able to speak, so she'd never heard his voice.

'How do you know he's such a gentleman then?' I pressed.

And she looked really puzzled.

'You know, I never realised he'd not actually spoken to me.' And then she smiled. 'There's just something about the way he conducts himself. It's in his eyes.'

And I knew exactly what she meant.

You know, I can picture Dad looking down on me just now and I can almost hear the words he would say: 'Mother of God, she doesn't half talk a load of bloody rubbish!'

OH STUFF IT!!

I need to tell you this one funny story and then I'll get back to what I'm supposed to be talking about, namely *working in radio*.

I've already told you that Dad was very shy; but he was also tremendously talented and creative. He was a master cabinetmaker and could turn his hand to anything. He even used to colour and perm Mum's hair; and such was his success that her friends used to queue up the stairs in the close on a Friday night to get him to tease their trestles.

He may have exaggerated this – it was the 60s and I have no way of verifying it. Mum always just nodded her head and agreed that this was gospel, but that counted for nothing. However, you know, it may well have been true, because given it was the 60s I imagine people were less fussy about their hair. Like most things in life, it's all relative.

When Dad lived in Dublin he was a well-known and well-respected cabinetmaker and ran his own small business. He also did upholstery and often went to people's homes to re-cover chairs, sofas, etc, in-situ. And it was on one such occasion that he did something that would have haunted me to my dying day had it been me, but which for some reason he found hilarious!

There he was in a grand house in a very posh suburb

of Dublin re-covering a sofa. The job took the whole day, and Dad was such a stickler for detail that everything would have had to have been just perfect or he wouldn't have left. But the lady of the house was terribly kind and made Dad his lunch, bringing it into him on a tray.

Now, I told you he was very shy, and good manners were everything to him. But Dad was also very fussy about his food. He didn't like anything... Well, he didn't like anything too... It's actually hard to say what he didn't like, but basically if our mum or his own Mammy hadn't cooked it then the dish would be viewed with the utmost suspicion.

There was nothing suspicious about the lunch he was served that day; it was obviously just disgusting. Or so he said. Mince and potatoes it was, swimming in grease, with soggy overcooked carrots mushed to the side of the plate. As soon as he looked at it his stomach churned. According to him the smell was even worse. He suspected that, despite the obvious display of wealth in the house, the meat was off.

He was mortified. How the hell could he get out of this? He'd already told the woman he was hungry and was about to nip out for a bite to eat. She'd asked him if he liked mince and potatoes and he had confirmed that it was his favourite. So now, faced with this rancid meal, he had no choice but to play around with it on his fork until she left him to eat it in peace.

By all accounts the lady of the house was rather

impressed that he would hardly stop for a spot of lunch and insisted on eating it 'on the hoof'. So she left him to it.

The unsightly greasy mess seemed to grow on the plate. One mouthful confirmed his worst fears – that the meat was indeed off – and that the whole thing was disgusting. He began to heave. It took every ounce of resolve not to be sick.

You really need to get inside the mind of that painfully shy person to understand the trauma this was now causing. He cast his eyes around the room, looking for some inconspicuous receptacle into which he could dump the offending meal.

But there was nothing, nowhere.

Giving her back the plate full of food was just not an option. Why had he taken this (bloody) job?

And then his eyes drifted towards the sofa; as yet unfinished and with a huge gaping chasm in the centre waiting to be stuffed with horse-hair and sewn back up.

You're probably one step ahead of me here! Yip, Dear Reader, you've guessed it. He scraped the mushy pile into the sofa and then, like a man possessed, frantically stretched the new fabric across the frame with absolute precision, sewed the whole thing back together, and ran like the clappers, the evidence concealed forever.

Recounting the story years later he could hardly keep a straight face. The tears of laughter often rolled down his cheeks. It was a mixture of embarrassment and just pure bloody relief that he had managed to pull it off. He left the house in an obvious hurry, never to return, and *'forgot'* to send the wifie the bill. And she in turn never pursued it.

Ironically, it was one of the best jobs he'd done. But then it *needed* to have been; there was no way he could have gone back to make adjustments!

And he always said it was the most expensive lunch he never ate.

GIVE THE HAMSTER A DOG
AND BONE...

I have already alluded to Mum being a real animal lover. Dad too loved animals, but I imagine he could have quite happily survived without them. (This does take quite a stretch of the imagination given that our house was always full of livestock, so I never quite got to see if this was in fact the case.)

In their twilight years, when all the weans – and the dog, the cat, the rabbit, the fish, the budgie and the terrapin – were away, our Parents relaxed into a life of retirement that involved babysitting, dogsitting, long walks and lunches. The house, instead of being quiet and restful, was even fuller than ever before. Them 'being at home all day with nothing to do' was brilliant. We could drop in anytime, and their house became a sort of Mecca for any friend, neighbour or passing shopkeeper who happened to have a day off. And folk thought nothing of dropping in with their dog in tow, or even leaving a wean or dog or cat to be looked after for a few hours.

Mum and Dad retired just before their first grandchild was born. Victoria was the apple of their eye. The night she was born was so wonderful and magical. We'd spent the entire day in the hospital, and when she eventually arrived it was the first time I'd ever seen my dad cry.

Anyway, their retirement coincided perfectly with this life-changing event and from there on in they were in charge of babysitting duties.

So it was no great surprise when I called one night and heard a really loud 'squeak' in the background.

'Ok,' I asked, 'who or what are you looking after now?'

'That's Hammy,' said Mum. 'We've got a hamster'

I had known it would only be a matter of time before they succumbed to getting a pet. I'd been hoping for a cat or maybe something more substantial, but a hamster was nice. That hamster seemed to grow louder and louder each night I phoned. 'He's settling in a treat,' yelled Mum, barely audible above the din of Hammy's squawking and the squeak of the wheel in his cage.

When I popped down for a visit shortly after, there was the brave Hammy. Bloody huge he was! And I swear he was jealous and actually bared his teeth when I approached.

'You do know that's a guinea pig and not a hamster?'

Neither of them seemed too bothered at this piece of news and went about their business.

'And he's very loud…'

Again they seemed unfazed by this. So as long as you didn't get too close or cosy with Hammy, and could tolerate the noise, he seemed harmless enough.

A few weeks passed without event, and then one day when I dropped by I couldn't help but notice an eerie silence. And an empty space where once Hammy had dwelled.

I was scared to ask. But felt I had to.

'What happened to Hammy then? Had he been sick? Was it all very sudden?'

'Swapped him for this,' Mum replied, holding up a state-of-the-art cordless phone.

'Eh?! Run that by me again.'

'Och, turns out your dad was allergic, and that nice chap in Tandy told me he couldn't think what to get his girlfriend for Valentine's Day, so...'

It transpires that my mum did indeed convince the hapless soul in the phone shop that his girlfriend would be cock-a-hoop with a hamster-cum-guinea pig. Mum not only convinced the sucker to take him off her hands, she even got a new phone as part of the deal!

CHILDREN – IF ONLY THEY'D JUST GROW UP!

I was walking behind a group of young girls on the way to work the other day. Well I was heading for work, the girls – no more than 11 or maybe 12 at a push – were going to school. They were walking five abreast with their arms folded, like a miniature mafia, creating quite a formidable barrier for anyone daring to cross their path.

For some reason one poor boy was the focus of their benign aggression and was really getting it in the neck. 'Him!' one of them remarked. 'Oh, don't get me started... he's *so* immature!'

As I ambled along with little purpose, I sympathised with the 12-year-old lad who had failed to grow up. He didn't have a hope in hell against this lot. And, as I walked past, a thought popped into my head that I never imagined I'd ever have, and that I fear may confirm I am truly middle aged: 'It was never like this in my day!'

I often wonder if that poor wee boy will ever catch up. Has the label, attached at such a young age, doomed him forever more to be 'immature'? I glanced into the future and could see his wife lobbying that very accusation across the breakfast table, with his as-yet-unborn children raising their eyes to heaven, aghast that their dad was just '*so* immature'. Perhaps the poor boy just wants to have some fun. He is only 12 after all.

But the labels pinned on us from an early age can last a lifetime.

THE GREAT GLASGOW WATERMELON SCANDAL AND ITS PART IN MY DOWNFALL!

I was once barred from my local Tesco Express.

Bloody cheek!

Well, it was more a self-imposed exile than an out and out ban. It was during a brief spell living in Glasgow city centre, and the said supermarket was the only shop within a 2 mile radius that sold anything other than kebabs. It was one momentary lapse in an otherwise exemplary life.

It was an unpleasant episode waiting to happen if you ask me. The assistant was wearing a badge that led me to believe she was 'happy to help'…yet it was obvious to anyone who looked that she was neither happy nor inclined to be helpful. I took the opportunity to point this out…which resulted in her becoming even less happy and even more disinclined to help, and in me being more annoyed.

I was in my pyjamas, which probably didn't help. It was pre-9am, so I considered the PJs to be fitting attire. Nobody had said anything about them all those years ago at Q96. (I wonder if any research has been conducted to establish the percentage of supermarket shoppers who enter the stores wearing their PJs? Just a thought.)

Anyway, the unpleasant exchange went something

like this:

Me: 'Can I have a plastic bag?'

Assistant: ......*nothing, just a steely gaze*

Me: 'Plastic bag please!'

Assistant: *still nothing*

Me: 'I didn't ask you for a flipping kidney, I just want a plastic bag!'

In my defence, I was very tired that morning and rather pissed off at something, though for the life of me I can't remember what. The assistant tutted loudly and shoved a poly bag in my direction.

But now I was having difficulty with the self-service till, which refused to scan my fruit.

'You really need to help me here,' I pleaded with The Unhelpful One.

In response, she let out the loudest sigh I have ever heard and said in her most patronising voice, 'You need to actually scan the bar-code,' then held the fruit aloft to ensure everyone could see that I was so stupid that I was unable to operate such a simple system.

In fairness to the grumpy assistant, the only other city dwellers who ventured out in their night clothes were the local Neds and seasoned drug users, so she was probably right to be on the defensive at the sight of me. As a Clarkston resident I often nipped over to the shops in my jammies. I had no idea that Neds had stolen my culture and were claiming it as their own.

So, amid the humiliation of being mistaken for a heroin

addict and all round eejit who couldn't buy a piece of fruit unaided, I sort of flipped.

'I'll tell you what…' I told her. My voice was getting louder and had reached the high-pitched screech of the hysterical. 'Stuff your fruit. I'm away to phone Glasgow Uni to tell them to take my degree back – on account that I'm clearly a bloody idiot or you wouldn't be speaking to me like this!'

Whereupon I ran off to shouts of, 'Don't you come back in here, we can do without your sorts.'

And it appeared that they could, since their business seemed to thrive thereafter. (However, as I write this they have recently issued a profits warning and are now being investigated by the Financial Conduct Authority. Cause and effect?)

Annoyingly, that meant I was forced to walk over a mile to buy a 3 kilo watermelon. I almost dislocated my shoulder carrying it back. However, on the way home I was handed a free tube of toothpaste by some student dentists promoting National Smile Week...the irony of which was not lost on me.

But you see, I was brought up in the age of the protest song, when it was considered quite respectable to complain. Life just wouldn't seem fair otherwise. I mean can you imagine Bob Dylan putting up with any of this? Or Marc Bolan for that matter? (Actually scrub that last reference, I've just read the lyrics to *Children of the Revolution* and they make no sense at all.)

And I'm not alone. Recently a friend of mine was barred from the Brighton Gay Bakery for a similar incident. It's happening all over you know.

Indeed across the globe middle-aged people are finding that what used to be regarded as a simple complaint is now frowned upon and considered a verbal assault in our world of Zero Tolerance.

William, my Welsh friend who runs a B&B in Italy, is barred from his local post office. After many years 'living the dream' in a tiny village on the outskirts of Lake Garda he eventually lost patience with the Italians' point-blank refusal to form an orderly queue. The poor man simply couldn't take it anymore. So William, being William, said something about it. He's terribly posh and assures me he chose his words very carefully. However, his remonstration apparently reduced a woman to tears... the very same woman who, just moments before, had plunged her elbow deep into William's solar plexus in an effort to gain advantage and get to the counter first.

As the locals rallied round to give this poor woman the comfort and succour she so clearly needed, William was banished from the shop and told never to darken its door again. He now has to walk 4 miles to post a letter.

But there is a bright side to this. William is 60 and secretly delighted at his bad boy reputation in the village; there's even talk of him buying a leather jacket. The whole thing has put a real spring in his step. (It's either that or his new hip.)

THE GOOD GIRL'S GUIDE TO THE PERFECT CHRISTMAS!

Someone pointed a finger at me last week and said, 'Oh Theresa doesn't do Christmas!'

Doesn't do Christmas! Blooming cheek.

Not only do I *Do Christmas*, I do it very well. In fact I love it. I love every single sparkly fun-filled minute of it.

Christmas is a great time. The planning, the preparation, the food, the drink, the excitement, the presents, the silly hats, the excess of cooking sherry, the enforced incarceration of distant relatives who can't stick each other... What's not to love?

Oh I *do* Christmas all right, make no mistake.

What I *don't* do is the pressure of Christmas. What I *don't* do is the stress of Christmas. What I *don't* do is talk about it from the first week in June so that when the actual day arrives my nerves are frazzled to a crisp and those chocolate Santas that seemed a rare bargain in August have melted onto the back of the drawer and only the dog or next door's weans can lick it clean. I do*n't* do any of that.

No! In our house – well in my *world* actually – this is the one thing I am most strict about and it's a deal breaker for anyone trying to enter my domain (whether or not they are using their Advance to Theresa, Pass Go and Collect

Two Hundred Pounds card).

On this matter my rules are clear. Nothing is allowed to happen until the 1st of December. Before then not one word is to be uttered regarding festivities, dinner, presents, seating plans or anything else that might trigger stress-markers. After the 1st we can talk about it until we're blue in the face. But since my family tend to produce their off-spring in December (I need to observe the mating habit of The Talbot more closely) there are a string of birthdays to absorb the Festive Chat.

For advice on having the best ever stress-free Christmas read on!

The tree goes up three or four days before the 'actual day'. I know you're breaking out in a cold sweat right now thinking this is horribly late, but go with me on this.

The tree should be a) real and b) the first one you see in the nursery or garden centre. Strike up a good relationship with the nursery throughout the year, and they'll always keep a nice special one by for you.

Remember, a good pair of secateurs, some decent pruning and good lighting can make even the scabbiest of trees look wonderful. While every other family in the street is up to its knees in pine needles, you will be transforming your house into a magical winter wonderland full of sparkles and twinkles. And while every other family in the street longs for Christmas to be over just so they can hoik their dried-out, withered old spruce off to the dump, you will have a luscious fresh tree full of perty greenness.

The smell of pine needles will intoxicate you and you will be chewing off your own knuckle with the anticipation of Christmas! Open a bottle of wine to quell this desire. Make it bubbly, to fit the occasion, as this feeling can be quite overwhelming and you'll be needing your knuckles later.

As the delicate bubbles dance on your tongue and you unravel your fairy lights – smugly, I might add – you'll wonder why everyone doesn't have the spiffing idea of wrapping the lights around a 12 x 12 inch piece of card the year before, thus ensuring they will never be tangled. (I find an old LP cover works best for this.)

With your tree now a testament to artistic perfection (the bottle of bubbly will make sure of this – I find everything looks better with a liberal dousing of champagne) it's time to do the Christmas Candles. Arm yourself with decent secateurs, a pair of loppers and a big wicker shopping basket and head outdoors for the necessary holly, ivy and any variegated foliage which tickles your fancy. If you don't have a garden, you may have to go further afield and forage for you foliage. Local parks (and, at a push, other people's gardens) are a good source of raw materials.

But please, Dear Reader, do check your local by-laws regarding drunk women brandishing sharp instruments at local bushes. And please read the disclaimer at the front of this book that says the publisher is NOT responsible for any act of violence or misconduct triggered by this publication. (I hope they've remembered to include it!)

Once it's been gathered, bung all the foliage in a sink full of water, along with blocks of oasis (magical green stuff you can buy from your local florist) and that'll keep it fresh until you're ready to work your magic.

But hang on, Theresa, won't I need my sink?

No. You won't be doing much cooking or cleaning so it's safe for the sink to be out of action for a day or so. You see, around this time of year I find it's best to either rely on carry-outs or just turn up randomly at friends' houses for the odd snack.

Once the artistic mood grips, stuff the well-soaked oasis with the foliage, add a massive church candle and some artificial flowers and voila – the perfect Christmas Candles!

But one word of warning. The candles cannot be lit until Christmas Eve. It's the rules.

As the day draws closer you'll realise that you will need some festive food. Happily, by this time you'll know how many to cater for. So get up nice and early on Christmas Eve – around 10am should do it – grab the best bottle of wine you can afford to part with and walk down to the local butchers, where they'll have your order all ready and made up per the instructions you gave over the phone on Dec 1st!

Next, pull up a seat (you might think of taking a fold-up one) and open the wine, and have a good chinwag with the butcher while sharing the wine with the stressed-out customers who are queuing out the door. (It's probably best not to share it with the butcher if he's still at the 'using the sharp knives' stage of his working day.)

On the way back up the road – and the key here is to ditch the car and buy a very snazzy shopping trolley – drop in to any local shops and buy whatever booze/fruit/ veg you may need. Remember, if they don't sell it, you don't need it. Again, get to know and support your local shopkeepers, and they'll make sure they look after you in times of stress! (Not that you will *be* stressing, of course, that's the whole point of this regime.)

Don't forget to give a hearty-yet-sympathetic wave to the now growing queue of miserable people stuck in an endless traffic jam on the way to or from some soulless shopping complex. You may wish to stop and pass the time of day with them. After all, they won't be going anywhere. That queue won't move for *at least* half an hour. However, don't be *too* smug. Remember, that was you last year!

Then it's time for the cinema. Admittedly you may need to revert to public transport or the car (though only if no alcohol was consumed earlier) for this one. Cinema tickets all round for *It's A Wonderful Life*, *Meet Me In St Louise* or *Miracle on 34th Street* wraps up any last-minute presents for siblings or any other relatives you may need to cater for.

Then it's back home to an immaculate house (while you were out the cleaners were in – make sure you put this on your Christmas wish list, you've got enough bath salts, thank you), with a sentimental tear in your eye, to light the Christmas Candles and have a romantic midnight supper. You may be on your own, but hey, who cares!

The next morning you'll be so filled with joy and love and wine and...eh, wine...that you will greet the day with all the excitement it deserves. And when your guests arrive jaded, exhausted and broken with the weight of Christmas, which has been on their shoulders since Good Friday, you will be the perfect host, a bon viveur ready to impart your good cheer to all who pass. For you, Christmas will be a welcome guest, greeted with open arms, with all the joy only a new love can bring.

'Genius!' I hear you say (albeit very quietly).

But believe you me, I too used to get stressed over Christmas. Or I was accused of getting other people stressed.

That accusation can only refer to one thing: The Ghost of Christmas Past. Or, more accurately, The Ghost of Christmas 1987...

THE UGLY GHOST
OF CHRISTMAS PAST!

"Twas the night before Christmas, when all through the house, not a creature was stirring...not even a mouse.'

(Clement C Moore back in 1822)

So you see, it *could* have all been so nice.

It was my first year in the cottage and I thought it would be wonderful to have my entire family over for Christmas Dinner. Food was always a big thing in our house; and, leaving nothing to chance, Mum had decided *she* would bring the turkey. A huge 20-pound affair. She would cook it that morning and she and Dad would bring it up for a further 10 minutes of basting in my oven. Then the big bird would 'rest' for the required 20 minutes, resulting in perfection. All *I* had to do was the veg and the starters. My sister would bring the puddings and various other tasks were assigned to various other family members.

I was beside myself with excitement – my first proper grown-up family Christmas, and I was in charge.

I think there were about 10 people for dinner that day, so the first task in the morning was to peel the spuds. My family love their tatties so it was a herculean task. I distinctly remember that Dumbo was on the telly-box. It's funny how little details like that stick in your mind years after an event.

My other half was appointed to spud duties and duly sat cross-legged on the living room floor in front of the aforementioned telly-box. He had a 10-stone bag of potatoes to one side of him, and in front was a pan of water the size of a small bath. He started peeling. He reckoned it might well be a messy job, so he covered the carpet with newspapers, saved his shower until later and just sat there unshaven in his boxers.

I was dancing around like a skittish horse, full of nerves and anticipation. The kitchen was a bit of a state from the excesses of Christmas Eve, but I had hours before everyone would arrive, so I stuck the dishwasher on and calculated I had more than enough time to get everything squared up. So I decided to have a wee snoozle on the settee, with Dumbo on in the background and the unshaven hippie peeling spuds on the floor.

I was just dozing off when the doorbell went. I just ignored it, hoping whoever it was would go away, but no luck, the bell-ringer was persistent. I shuffled off to answer the door, still in my dressing gown, hair like a burst mattress and the previous night's mascara snaking down my cheeks. I hadn't even had time to open the curtains.

I will never forget the sight that greeted me. There, standing en masse, was my entire family, dressed up like a band-box, groaning under the weight of food and drink and presents. Dad was straining to carry the 20-pound bird in a huge basket. It was still cooking, with steam belching from every corner.

I was younger then and not much fazed me. I looked them up and down.

'You're a bit early,' I said, hoping they would go away and come back at a more civilised hour.

My Mother tried to speak but no words came. I was glad of that.

'It's 2 o'clock!!!' my sister screamed.

'Exactly,' I replied. 'I wasn't expecting you until... around 6ish???'

They refused to go, more or less (actually, it was definitely *more*) barging their way into the living room, with its spuds and boxer-shorted hippie and closed curtains and *Dumbo*.

It was then that my Mother regained her power of speech. And let me tell you, Dear Reader, what she said wasn't very nice.

Then Dad pitched in. 'Jesus, Mary and Joseph! You've ruined Christmas!'

It was then and only then that Mum snapped into action.

'Not on your bloody nelly,' she replied. Then she did what she did best: took charge. 'You,' she said to my dad, who was now in a state of apoplexy, clutching the still-cooking turkey to his breast like a life-jacket, 'kitchen!' And from there on she snapped her fingers and barked an instruction to each and every one of us.

The hippy was still cross-legged on the floor, peeling

his way through the mountain of potatoes. 'Just leave him,' she said, 'he's the only one doing any bloody work.'

And so it came to pass that within 20 minutes the kitchen was cleaned, the table set, the veg cooked and the starters laid out. Just enough time for the precious cooked bird to rest and to allow the natural juices to be absorbed into the now succulent meat.

I don't think there ever was a better Christmas dinner than the one Mum threw together in a flash. My sister has some vague recollection of opening the deep fat fryer (very big in the '80s) to make cheat's roast potatoes to save time and being met by a rogue mushroom left over from a Halloween dinner party. Apparently it was cultivating its own eco-system in a sea of fungus. But I think she made that up.

It is since then that I've realised you don't need months and months of planning to have the best-ever Christmas day. All you need is the sort of determination that my mum displayed in that time of adversity.

And there's not a day goes by that I don't miss her.

SCOTLAND THE BRAVE?
MIBEES AYE MIBEES NAW!

It's Wednesday night and I have the familiar tight knot in my stomach that doesn't just *say* 'pre-exam nerves', it *screams* it like a claxon designed to waken the dead. Tomorrow's test is relatively easy; multiple choice and just one question: *'Should Scotland be an independent country?'*

How the hell should I know? I'm not even sure if I have a very strong sense of National Identity, whatever that is. I've never had to think about it before.

If I'm honest I feel more Glaswegian than Scottish or British. But it seems to be an affliction of 'city folk' that we're not as Scottish or as Irish or as Welsh as our country cousins.

Or maybe it's my background. My parents were both from Dublin – again, city folk – so perhaps their own national identifies were diluted somewhat and this was passed on to us, be it intentional or otherwise. They came over here in the '50s, possibly on their way to somewhere else, and just sort of stayed. So in truth I'm an accidental Glaswegian. I could so easily have been a Mancunian, a Brummie or even an 'apples and pears, Missus' Londoner, with pearly buttons sewn onto my clothes and a promise to call you up on the dog and bone to spout no end of other wonderful cocker-ney rhyming slang.

But no, I'm Glaswegian. Or, to be more precise if filling out one of those long-winded pointless forms that ask you for your race, religion and ethnicity, I'm a Glaswegian Catholic, which means I had to go to mass until I was 16 and by default sort of supported Celtic (unless they're wearing that appalling 'away strip'; they don't deserve my support then! But now my friend's son is a professional footballer so I follow whatever team he plays for. At the time of writing I'm a Hull supporter!)

I have friends of Irish descent who are much more 'Irish' than I am. I've met people from Wales who promise to keep a welcome in the hillside if ever I happen to be passing, and Scottish colleagues who wear the kilt with pride and can name every member of the Jacobite Rebellion, tracing their ancestors back centuries; whereas I get as far as 1963 and then I'm struggling.

And is National Pride always such a good thing? I have a friend who was at primary school in the late '60s. Apparently a shortage of teachers saw several old biddies wheeled out of retirement to mop up the demand. Alas he was landed with one such firebrand who was actually born during the reign of Queen Victoria (as with Lionel Blair earlier, Google her if you're under 50!). She insisted on her 7-year-old charges standing up each morning and belting out either the National Anthem or *Rule Britannia*. Anyone who didn't give it the passion it deserved was wrapped across the knuckles with a ruler (not the Victorian monarch kind!). I'm not sure that behaviour would be allowed today.

So what will tomorrow's referendum bring? Will a vote for Independence mean we'll still have a BBC Scotland… with, may I add, local travel bulletins? Should I even bother setting my alarm for the coming months? Will I need a new passport? (Because I'm telling you this, I'm not having another nightmare mug shot taken if I do. I'd be better getting a police artist to sketch an impression of me.) Will we be swimming in a sea of free Irn Bru, up to our oxters in oil, basking in the wealth the revenue should have been bringing in this past half a century?

Or will we wake up on Friday morning with the same old same old. Still stuck to Blighty like an old comfy pair of slippers, mortified that we kicked up such a fuss in the first place? And if we agree that we are indeed 'Better Together' will I have to support England in the World Cup?

And answer me this: will we ever be able to sing *Flower of Scotland* with pride again at another Scotland rugby match, belting out the line '…and we can still rise now and be a nation again…'? Would we be laughed out of the stadium?

Who knows? Can't get a decent bloody answer from either side.

So I have no idea why I'm so nervous about tomorrow's test. It's not as though I can get the answer wrong – it's just my opinion after all. And what difference will my one opinion make?

I've never known a single vote or election or referendum polarise opinion as much as the one on September 18th 2014. I've seen best friends fall out over it, I've witnessed family feuds. I myself was accused of having a 'loser mentality' because I questioned whether or not we could indeed 'go it alone' – a question I was perfectly entitled to ask, just as I also asked if staying within the UK was a good idea given that this will probably be the only chance in our lifetimes to cast such a vote and gain our freedom. That brought ridicule and sniggers from the other side, as my question obviously conjured up images of blue-faced Hollywood rebels with mid-Atlantic accents. That Mel Gibson has a lot to answer for.

Now, I'm a huge fan of the philosopher John Stuart Mill. He believed that every fact, every opinion, should be open for debate 'or it will be held as a dead dogma and not a living truth'. According to Mill, in order to make the right decision we must use discussion and experience.

We often hear of bad losers, but you can get bad winners too. It would be awful if the winning side gloated so much at its apparent victory that the opposing voters felt disenfranchised, their voices not heard.

And now it seems that the referendum has sparked a renewed vigour in separatist movements across Europe. Those in Spain, Belgium and Italy have seized the political mood to reignite their own goals. Is it any wonder I'm nervous? My single vote could be responsible for Italy losing the heel of her boot forever – or, perhaps worse, for it to be stuck there for eternity like a big noisy metal seg! I feel the ghost of Garibaldi breathing down my neck.

I'm not going to say where my allegiance shall lie, because in truth it lies with each and every person in Scotland. Because no matter what the outcome, we've displayed a level of political motivation unprecedented in my lifetime at least. As a nation we've become galvanised in our belief that the political future of our country is in our hands. We're in charge of this one, thank you very much. This is way too important to leave to the politicians.

So there should be no winners and no losers in tomorrow's referendum. Should it transpire that as a nation we vote to stay in the United Kingdom, then that decision should be accepted with a desire and a renewed vigour, knowing we all have a part to play. And if indeed we are to become an independent nation again, then we should move forward to create a brand new Scotland with all the vitality and energy and vigour that only youth can bring.

By the time you read this we'll know the outcome... and a whole new chapter of life will have begun.